Use
Your
Computer

By
Ron Fry

CAREER PRESS
3 Tice Road
P.O. Box 687
Franklin Lakes, NJ 07417
1-800-CAREER-1
201-848-0310 (NJ and outside U.S.)
FAX: 201-848-1727

USE YOUR COMPUTER

ISBN 1-56414-235-3, $6.99

Cover design by The Visual Group

Printed in the U.S.A. by Book-mart Press

To order this title by mail, please include price as noted above, $2.50 handling per order, and $1.00 for each book ordered. Send to: Career Press, Inc., 3 Tice Road, P.O. Box 687, Franklin Lakes, NJ 07417.

Or call toll-free 1-800-CAREER-1 (NJ and Canada: 201-848-0310) to order using VISA or MasterCard, or for further information on books from Career Press.

Library of Congress Cataloging-in-Publication Data

Fry, Ronald W.
    Use your computer / by Ron Fry.
      p.   cm. -- (Ron Fry's how to study program)
    Includes index.
    ISBN 1-56414-235-3 (paper)
    1. Microcomputers.   I. Series: Fry, Ronald W. How to study program.
QA76.5.F769 1996
004.16'024375--dc20   96-16333
                                           CIP

Contents

Foreword

Enter your password

A number of you are students, not just the high school students I always thought were my readers, but college students (a rousing plug for their high school preparation) and *junior* high students (which says something far more positive about their motivation and eventual success).

Many of you are adults. Some of you are returning to school, and some of you are long out of school, but if you could learn *now* the study skills your teachers never taught, you'd do better in your careers (especially if you knew how to utilize online services to write an attention-getting memo or deliver a raise-making presentation).

All too many of you are parents with the same lament: "How do I get Johnny to do better in school? He knows a lot more about computers than I do, but spends four hours a day 'chatting' online."

I want to briefly take the time to address every one of the audiences for this book and discuss some of the factors particular to each of you:

If you're a high school student

You should be particularly comfortable with both the language and format of this book—its relatively short sentences and paragraphs, occasionally humorous (hopefully) headings and subheadings, a reasonable but certainly not outrageous vocabulary. I wrote it with you in mind! While you may already be computer-literate, you'll need to learn a lot more than just "the basics" to do well in school. And if you're planning to go on to college, I guarantee you *must* master these skills.

If you're a junior high school student

You are trying to learn how to study at *precisely* the right time. Sixth, seventh and eighth grades—before that sometimes cosmic leap to high school—are without a doubt the period in which all these study skills should be mastered. Unless you're just learning about computers, I doubt you'll have trouble with the concepts or the language.

If you're a "traditional" college student...

...somewhere in the 18 to 25 age range, you must master all the skills in this book to thrive, let alone survive, in the competitive collegiate environment. If you don't know a bit from a byte, do not pass "Go." Do not go on a date. Take the time to learn these skills now.

What can parents do?

There are probably even more dedicated parents out there than dedicated students, since the first phone call at any of my radio or TV appearances comes from a sincere and worried parent asking, "What can I do to help my kid do better in school?" Okay, here they are, the rules for parents of students of any age:

1. **Set up a homework area.** Free of distraction, well lit, all necessary supplies handy.
2. **Set up a homework routine.** When and where it gets done. Same bat-time every day.
3. **Set homework priorities.** Actually, just make the point that homework *is* the priority—before a date, before TV, before going out to play, etc.
4. **Make reading a habit**—for them, certainly, but also for yourselves. Kids will inevitably do what you *do*, not what you *say* (even if you say *not* to do what you *do*).
5. **Turn off the TV.** Or, at the very least, severely limit when and how much TV-watching is appropriate. This may be the toughest one. Believe me, I'm the father of a 7-year old. I know. Do your best.
6. **Talk to the teachers.** Find out what your kids are supposed to be learning. If you don't, you can't really supervise.
7. **Encourage and motivate**, but don't nag them to do their homework. It doesn't work.
8. **Supervise their work**, but don't fall into the trap of *doing* their homework.
9. **Praise them to succeed**, but don't overpraise them for mediocre work. Be wary of any school or teacher more worried about your kid's "self esteem" than her grades, skills and abilities.
10. **Convince them of reality.** This is for older students. It's almost as much of a stretch as turning off the TV, but learning that the real world won't care about their grades but measure them by what they know and what they can do will save many tears (probably yours).

11. **If you can afford it, get your kid(s) a computer** and all the software they can handle. Many people have been saying it for years (including me) and there really is no avoiding it: Your kids, whatever their age, absolutely must master computers in order to succeed in school and after school.

The importance of your involvement

Don't for a minute underestimate the importance of *your* commitment to your child's success: Your involvement in your child's education is absolutely essential to his or her eventual success. Surprisingly enough, the results of every study done in the last two decades about what affects a child's success in school clearly demonstrate that only one factor *overwhelmingly* affects it, every time: parental involvement. Not the size of the school, the money spent per pupil, the number of language labs, how many of the students go on to college, how many great teachers there are (or lousy ones). All factors, yes. *But none as significant as the effect you can have.*

And you can help tremendously, *even if you were not a great student yourself, even if you never learned great study skills,* even if you don't even know how to turn your kid's computer on! You can learn now with your child—not only will it help him or her in school, it will help *you* on the job, whatever your field.

If you're a nontraditional student

If you're going back to high school, college or graduate school at age 25, 45, 65 or 85—you probably need the help the nine books in my *How to Study Program* offer more than anyone! Why? Because the longer you've been out of school, the more likely you don't remember what you've forgotten. As much as I emphasize that it's rarely too early to learn good study habits, I must also emphasize that it's never too *late*.

If you're returning to school and attempting to carry even a partial load of courses while simultaneously holding down a job, raising a family, or both, there are some particular problems you face that you probably didn't the first time you were in school:

Time and money pressures. Let's face it, when all you had to worry about was going to school, it simply *had* to be easier than going to school, raising a family and working for a living simultaneously. (And it was!)

Self-imposed fears of inadequacy. You may well convince yourself that you're just "out of practice" with all this school stuff. You don't even remember what to do with a highlighter! While some of this fear is valid, most is not. The valid part is that you are returning to an academic atmosphere, one that you may not have even visited for a decade or two. And it *is* different (which I'll discuss more below) than the "work-a-day" world. That's just a matter of adjustment and, trust me, it will take a matter of days, if not hours, to dissipate. But I suspect many of you are fearing that you just aren't in that school "mentality" anymore, that you don't "think" the same way.

These last fears are groundless. You've been out there thinking and doing for quite a few years, perhaps very successfully, so it's really ridiculous to think school will be so different. It won't be. Relax.

Feeling you're "out of your element." This is a slightly different fear, the fear that you just don't fit in any more. After all, you're not 18 again. But then, neither are half the college students on campus today. That's right, fully 50 percent of all college students are older than 25. The reality is, you'll probably feel more in your element now than you did the first time around!

You'll see teachers differently. Probably a plus. It's doubtful you'll have the same awe you did before. At worst, you'll consider teachers your equals. At best, you'll consider them younger and not necessarily as successful or experienced as you are.

There *are* differences in academic life. It's slower than the "real" world, and you may well be moving significantly faster than its normal pace. Despite your own hectic schedule, do not expect campus life to accelerate in response. You will have to get used to people and systems with far less interest in speed.

Some random thoughts about learning

Learning shouldn't be painful and certainly doesn't have to be boring, though it's far too often both. However, it's not necessarily going to be wonderful and painless, either. Sometimes you actually have to work hard to figure something out or get a project done. That *is* reality.

It's also reality that everything isn't readily apparent or easily understandable. That confusion reigns. Tell yourself that's okay and learn how to get past it. As any computer nut will confirm, there's a lot of trial and error in Netland. I guarantee you'll make some mistakes along the way.

Heck, if you actually think you understand everything the first time through, you're kidding yourself. Learning slowly doesn't mean there's something wrong with you. A good student doesn't panic when something doesn't seem to be getting through the haze. He just takes his time, follows whatever steps apply and remains confident that the light bulb will indeed inevitably go off.

There are other study guides

Though I immodestly maintain my *How to Study Program* to be the most helpful to the most people, there are lots of other purported study books out there (though as far as I know *none* of them deal with the specifics included in *this* book). Unfortunately, I don't think many deliver what they promise. In fact, I'm getting mad at the growing number of study guides out there claiming to be "the sure way to straight As" or something of the sort. These are also the books that dismiss reasonable alternative ways to study and learn with, "Well, that never worked for me," as if that is a valid reason to dismiss it, as if we should *care* that it didn't work for the author.

Inevitably, these books promote the authors' "system," which usually means what *they* did to get through school. This "system," whether basic and traditional or wildly quirky, may or may not work for you. So what do you do if "their" way of taking notes makes no sense to you? Or you master their highfalutin "Super Student Study Symbols" and still get Cs?

I'm not getting into a Dennis Miller rant here, but there are very few "rights" and "wrongs" out there in the study world. There's certainly no single "right" way to attack a multiple choice test or absolute "right" way to take notes. So don't get fooled into thinking there *is*, especially if what you're doing seems to be working for you. Don't change what "ain't broke" because some self-proclaimed study guru claims what you're doing is all wet. Maybe he's all wet. After all, if his system works for you, all it *really* means is you have the same likes, dislikes, talents or skills as the author.

Needless to say, don't read *my* books looking for the Truth—that single, inestimable system of "rules" that works for everyone. You won't find it, 'cause there's no such bird.

You *will* find a plethora of techniques, tips, tricks, gimmicks and what-have-you, some or all of which may work for you, some of which won't. Pick and choose, change and adapt, figure out what works for you. Because *you* are responsible for creating *your* study system, *not me*.

Yes, I'll occasionally point out my way of doing something. I may even suggest that I think it offers some clear advantages to all the alternative ways of accomplishing the same thing. But that *doesn't* mean it's some carved-in-stone, deviate-from-the-sacred-Ron-Fry-study-path-under-penalty-of-a-writhing-death kind of rule.

I've used the phrase "Study smarter, not harder" as a sort of catch-phrase in promotion and publicity for the **How to Study Program** for nearly a decade. So what does it mean to you? Does it mean I guarantee you'll spend less time studying? Or that the least amount of time is best? Or that studying isn't *ever* supposed to be hard?

Hardly. It means that studying inefficiently is wasting time that could be spent doing other (okay, probably more *fun)* things and that getting your studying done as quickly and efficiently as possible is a realistic, worthy and *attainable* goal. I'm no stranger to hard work, but I'm not a monastic dropout who thrives on self-flagellation. I try not to work harder than I have to!

I can guarantee that the nearly 1,200 pages of my **How to Study Program** contain the most wide-ranging, comprehensive, up-to-date and complete system of studying ever published. I have attempted to create a system that is usable, that is useful, that is practical, that is learnable. One that *you* can use—whatever your age, whatever your level of achievement, whatever your IQ—to start doing better in school, in work and in life *immediately*.

Ron Fry
May 1996

Chapter 1

Computers are a student's best friend

In 1986, Apple Computer, Inc. equipped seven elementary and secondary schools in various parts of the country with computers. The idea was to find out whether or not having the latest technology at hand would change the ways students learned.

Ten years later, the students were mastering basic skills 30 percent faster than before, scoring 10 percent to 15 percent higher on standardized tests, writing more and with more fluidity, staying in school longer and showing a greater inclination to go on to college.

Not only that, they seemed more excited about learning in general, more confident that they *could* learn and more likely to work with their fellow students. Apple's "Classrooms of Tomorrow" program showed that while computers can't turn every student into an Einstein, they can make learning more interesting and more challenging by offering new ways to learn and putting virtually unlimited resources at the students' fingertips.

Of course, the average high school or college student has not been totally immersed in computer technology, as were the youngsters in the Classrooms of Tomorrow. But many have access to computers at home or at school. Most high schools and colleges make computers available to their students in the library or in computer rooms, and some colleges require every incoming student to have a computer.

Whether you have the latest high-tech equipment or an old clunker sitting on your desk, you can use your computer to increase your skills, expand your knowledge and make research simple. Your computer can help you to:

- Brush up your English skills.
- Increase and test your knowledge of mathematics, including algebra and geometry.
- Listen to native speakers pronouncing words in the language you are studying.
- Research issues in numerous encyclopedias, dictionaries and other reference sources.
- Get information on abortion, civil rights and other issues from organizations involved.
- Travel down the Amazon River, visit ancient Greek ruins or the site of a concentration camp.
- Read classical literature and philosophy in its original language or in English.
- "Dissect" the human body or watch as a virus invades a body cell.
- Pose questions to other students or professionals in the field you are studying.

- Study paintings in the Louvre and many other museums around the world.
- Read abstracts and complete articles from professional journals published around the world.
- Study the Declaration of Independence, the text of Dr. Martin Luther King's "I Have a Dream" speech or all of the presidential inauguration speeches.
- View blueprints of significant buildings.
- Practice for the SAT, GRE and other important tests.
- Leave messages for and get information from the President of the United States, congressmen, senators, Supreme Court justices and other government officials.
- See the stars and the planets through the "eyes" of spacecraft, satellites and probes.
- Study time lines of history, literature, physics and just about any other subject.

And once you've gathered all that information, you can use word processing programs such as Microsoft Word or WordPerfect to correct your spelling and grammar, to help you find more interesting words to use and to prepare professional-looking documents complete with italicized and boldfaced type, columns and inserts.

For math or accounting projects, you can use spreadsheet programs such as Excel or Lotus 1-2-3 to organize and manipulate data, and to prepare charts and graphs that illustrate the main points you want to make.

Database programs, which help you keep track of large bodies of information, can make gathering and organizing information for a paper a breeze. Graphics programs help even the artistically challenged sketch out drawings and plans. Multimedia programs that combine text, video, sound and pictures can help you present what you've learned in a dynamic, compelling manner.

With various word processing, spreadsheet, database, graphics and multimedia programs, with educational and special-topic programs, with access to online and Internet services, the computer-aided student has a definite leg up in the race to educational success.

Computers won't study for you or make you smarter, but they can make learning much more enjoyable, efficient and productive.

Chapter 2 offers a brief explanation of what makes a computer tick—we'll take a quick look under the computer's "hood." Chapter 3 gives tips for buying a computer. Chapter 4 discusses some popular educational software. Chapters 5, 6 and 7 examine educational possibilities on the Information Superhighway. Chapter 8 is a glossary of computer terms you should know.

Chapter 2

Inside the computer

Using a computer is like having a dialogue. It's a one-way dialogue, if you will, with you asking questions and issuing orders, and your talking partner responding without complaint. It's a great way of communicating except for two small drawbacks: You and your partner speak totally different languages, and neither of you hears what the other is saying. It's these little problems that make computers seem so mysterious and difficult to use. But remember: Operating your computer is just like having a chat with a friend. All that hardware—those boxes, hard drives, chips, ports, busses, expansion slots, the screen, the keyboard and the mouse—are only there to make that simple little conversation possible.

Let's take a brief look "under the hood," just enough to get an idea of how we humans can have productive conversations with our computers.

You and your CPU

Your talking partner is the computer's *central processing unit,* also called the *microprocessor, processor* or *CPU.*

The CPU is the heart of the computer, the place where the critical computing work is done. Many people describe it as the computer's brain, but that analogy is a little misleading, for it implies that the CPU can actually think and make decisions. It can't. The only thing a CPU does is process information—which is why it's called a central *processing* unit. It doesn't think, dream or make decisions. It just processes. But it does juggle a staggering amount of information at speeds too fast for us to comprehend.

386, 486—What?

When you purchase a computer, or talk to computer users, you'll hear lots of numbers, such as "386" and "486." These refer to the CPUs (central processing units), which are given numbers, not names, at birth. The higher the number, the newer and presumably better the CPU. Not too long ago, the CPU known as "80286" (pronounced "eighty, two eighty-six) or "286" (pronounced "two eighty-six") for short, was state-of-the-art for IBM and IBM-compatible computers. Soon, of course, the 80286 was improved and given a new name, 100 points above the old: "80386," or "386" for short. Then it underwent more modifications, and was renamed the "80486," or "486."

The 486 was upgraded and should have been called the "80586," or "586." But Intel, the company that makes these chips, decided to give the new CPU a real name, because a number can't be patented. So the numbering system was dropped and the "586" was officially dubbed the "Pentium."

If you want to touch your CPU, you'll find it on a little silicon chip inside the big box that we normally call "the computer." The CPU consists of millions of tiny electronic switches, or transistors, much too small for the human eye to see unaided. There are other electronic gizmos on the chip, such as the *bus interface unit,* the *data cache* and the *branch predictor unit.* They all exist to serve the electronic switches, and are never given a single thought by the average computer user.

Speed and power

There are other ways to measure a CPU's performance, other than by its number. You can also look at its speed and power.

Each CPU chip operates at a set speed—the faster it runs, the more it will cost you. CPU speed is measured in *megahertz,* or *MHz* for short. The higher the MHz, the better. Today, home computers that run at 133 MHz or more are considered speedy.

Keep in mind that chips with the same names can have different speeds. There are Pentium chips that dash along at 133 MHz, and those that jog behind at only 75 MHz. Computer advertisements often say something like "133 MHz/Pentium," giving both the chip name/number and the speed.

A CPUs ability to handle information is also limited by its *bit width,* which refers to how many bits of information it can handle at a time. The bigger the number, the more bits it can bite into at once. A 32-bit processor, the industry standard today, can chew into information twice as fast as a 16-bit processor.

Six zeros and two ones spell "A"?

The only language computers understand is a binary language, and one consisting of only two "letters": "1" and "0," also known as "on" and "off."

Whereas English uses the 26 letters of the alphabet to create words, sentences and paragraphs, binary computer language uses only the "1" and "0," the "on" and the "off," to do the same.

I mentioned earlier that the CPU is filled with tiny electronic switches. If electricity is flowing through one of those many switches, that switch is "on." If electricity is *not* flowing through a switch, it's switch is "off."

Each switch contains one bit of information ("1" or "0"). But since we deal with information much more complex than "1" and "0," many bits must be grouped together before any useful work can be done. After all, how could you possibly represent the 26 letters of the English alphabet, plus the numerals, the comma, the period, the quotation mark and other characters, with just a "1" or a "0"?

That's why the CPU groups bits together, to represent more complex information.

A byte—which is eight little bits in a row—is really the smallest piece of information we normally talk about. For example, a byte made up of these consecutive 8 bits—01000001—stands for the letter "A."

Little bytes and big bytes

The word "bit" was coined when someone squashed together the two words "*bi*nary dig*it*."

8 bits = 1 byte

1,024 bytes = 1 kilobyte

1,000,000 kilobytes = 1 megabyte

1,000,000,000 megabytes = 1 gigabyte

All the time you're working on your computer, the CPU is throwing the electronic switches on and off at breathtaking speed, constantly changing "1s" to "0s" and vice versa in order to process information. That's all the CPU does—manipulate millions of switches at blinding speed, with each switch representing one little bit of information.

All the other stuff

Clearly, people and CPUs cannot communicate directly. We don't pick up the CPU and talk to it. And we can't even see, let alone understand, what the computer is "saying" by squinting at millions of "on" and "off" switches. Bits and bytes mean nothing to us. This means that we need translators to transform English into binary computer language and back again. We also need other devices to serve as eyes, ears, mouths, pencils and crayons, allowing us to "see" and "hear" each other.

That's what all the stuff surrounding the little CPU does.

Talking and talking back

Before looking at the translators that turn English into computer language and vice versa, let's take a quick look at the devices that allow us to "talk" to the CPU and the little chip to "talk" back.

Anything you "say" to your CPU is *input*. We usually do that with the most popular of input devices, the keyboard. Keyboards are fairly standard devices, with the main bank of keys looking just like those on a typewriter, often another set of keys off to the right looking like the keys on an adding machine and a long row of keys toward the top of the board. Typing on the keyboard sends electronic impulses to the CPU, which interprets them and manipulates its transistor switches appropriately.

The *mouse* is a little box with a ball peeking out from the bottom. When you move your mouse around on your desk the ball rolls around. Each movement of the ball causes an arrow or other representation of the mouse to move around on your screen. When you get the arrow to where you want it to be, you can push one or more buttons on the mouse to make different things happen. The *track-ball* is essentially an upside down mouse, with the ball protruding up out of the box. Instead of pushing the mouse around to make the ball inside move, you simply roll the ball itself.

Ports have nothing to do with boats

A *port* is a hole in the back of your computer where you can plug in input and output devices. The printer is plugged into the *printer port,* the hard discs and scanners in the *SCSI* port and so on. It's usually pretty obvious what gets plugged where, because many of the plugs are only designed to fit into specific holes, and because the holes often have little pictures above them, telling you what belongs there.

You'll hear the terms *serial port* and *parallel port* a lot. In a serial port, information moves single file, bit by bit, through one-way wires (like cars on a one-way road). Incoming information comes in on one wire, outgoing information moves out on another. In a parallel port, the information travels side by side over many wires, eight bits of information lined up and moving through multiple wires simultaneously (like cars on an eight-lane superhighway).

SCSI, which is pronounced "scuzzy," stands for Small Computer System Interface. A scuzzy port is a speedy, flexible serial port.

A *joystick,* like the ones on video games in the arcades, is another input device, as are special tablets and pens. Even your finger can be an input device, if the computer is able to recognize and interpret finger touches to the screen.

Scanners and *digital cameras* allow us to put images into the CPU. And for that matter, *discs* and *disc drives* are also specialized input devices. We'll talk more about them shortly.

A *modem* is a special kind of combined input/output device. Special because we can't use it for direct human-to-CPU communication. Instead, modems allow computers to "talk" to each other over the phone wires. But since we control what goes through the modem, it qualifies as both an input and an output device.

We use input devices to talk to the CPU, and the little chip talks back to us through *output* devices such as screens, printers and speakers. These devices allow the CPU to put the information out in forms we can see and hear.

A quick look at monitors

For all practical purposes, you can think of your computer monitor as being pretty much like a TV screen.

You want the images your monitor produces to be sharply focused, or (in computer lingo) to have "high resolution." Good resolution depends on having plenty of little dots of light, called *pixels,* on the monitor's screen.

Although a single pixel, which stands for *picture element,* may be created by multiple points of light, we normally think of a pixel as being one dot of light.

The more pixels on a screen, the smaller each dot of light and the better the resolution. Pixels are arranged in rows and columns on the screen. If your screen is described as having 700 by 500, it means that there are 700 columns and 500 rows of pixels, totaling 350,000 pixels.

Translators and order-givers

Input and output devices make it easy for humans and CPUs to "talk" to each other. But there's one more problem to overcome: We don't speak the same language—not even close. That's why we need translators to convert English into the binary language of computers and back again.

There is no single translator in the computer. Instead the translating is done in various ways at different levels. The most important translator that the typical computer user deals with is *software*. Not only does software translate, it also issues detailed instructions to the computer.

There are two general types of software: *application software* and *operating system software*. Application software, typically called *programs,* includes word processing programs, data bases, spread sheets and games.

Let's say, for example, that you want to write a letter. You certainly know that you want to type in "Dear Bob: How are you?" and so on. What you probably don't know is that you also have to tell the computer how to set up paragraphs, how to center your stationary at the top of the page, how to number each page, how to alphabetize the list of names you're including in the letter, how to run a spelling check and so on.

Fortunately, word processing programs such as Word-Perfect or Microsoft Word issue all of those instructions for you in a language the CPU understands. They also instruct the CPU to show an image of a piece of paper on the screen as you type your letter, to make the letters appear on the screen as soon as you type them, to make them boldfaced, italicized and/or underlined at your command and to have the printer print out a copy of the letter when you're ready for it.

Overall order givers

Application programs are specialized translators and order givers with specific tasks, such as word processing.

The other type of software, operating system software, is assigned the more generalized task of running both the CPU and the software. The operating software acts as the organizer for the entire computer.

The three most popular pieces of system software are:

- Mac OS, the **Mac**intosh **o**perating **s**ystem used in Macintosh computers.

- DOS, which stands for **d**isc **o**perating **s**ystem, and is used to run IBM and IBM-compatible computers.

- Windows, a relatively new operating system that "sits on top of" DOS in IBM and IBM-compatible computers.

Each of the three main operating systems has fierce partisans and foes. Generally speaking:

- The Macintosh operating system is the easiest to learn and use, but can only be used on Macintosh computers, which are more expensive than the average home computer. And fewer programs have been written for the Macintosh, so you have less of a choice.

- DOS, which used to be the most popular operating system for home computers, is harder to learn. On the other hand, many programs have been written for DOS, and the IBM-compatible computers that run DOS are less expensive than the Macintoshes.

- Windows, which is used in conjunction with DOS, makes IBM and IBM-compatible computers look and act almost as "friendly" as Macintoshes.

There are other operating systems, such as UNIX and OS/2, but they're relatively rare in the popular computer market. We'll talk more about Macintosh and IBM-type computers in Chapter 3.

Assisting the CPU

The CPU needs help to run the highly complex modern computer. It gets that help from assistants called *coprocessors* which may be found in the printer, keyboard and other strategic parts of the computer.

The *math coprocessor* is a specially designed processor that handles calculations. You don't have to have a math coprocessor unless you're using spreadsheet, math or design programs that process lots of numbers. Newer CPUs, however, have built-in math coprocessors.

There are also coprocessors in keyboards, printers, video cards and other parts of the computer to handle special, limited tasks without having to "bother" the CPU.

Remembering it all—temporarily

The CPU itself has a very limited ability to remember things, so it must store data elsewhere. Most of that information is put into "deep storage," but some has to be kept close at hand. Actually, it could all be kept in the deep storage room, but then the CPU would have to waste time running back and forth to retrieve it. Keeping the pertinent facts close at hand, in "quick storage," saves a lot of time.

The computer's quick storage room is called *random access memory,* or *RAM* for short. When you open a program or begin working on a document, the CPU takes the relevant information out of deep storage and places it into RAM, where it can be rapidly manipulated. Anything you type into the computer is also placed into RAM (at first).

Whenever necessary, the CPU gets more information out of deep storage, or puts temporary RAM information into permanent deep storage. The CPU also manipulates the data in RAM.

Because RAM information is created by bursts of electricity flipping tiny switches, RAM is erased once the electricity goes off. Whatever has not been transferred back to deep storage is gone forever. (There are new forms of RAM which can hold information after the computer has been turned off. Most home computers today, however, have electricity-dependent RAM.)

Remembering it all—forever

RAM is quick and easy to get to, but short-lived. Once you pull the plug, it's gone. Naturally, we need a permanent form of memory, someplace to store the documents we write, the graphics we design, the spread sheets we set up to track our financial progress and the thousands of names we've typed into the data bases. Without permanent storage, we'd constantly need to recreate our work. We'd also have to type all the instructions that make up a program into the computer before we could use it. We need a deep storage memory that lasts, well, if not forever, at least for a very long time.

Discs and *hard drives* provide that permanent storage. All of our work, plus anything else we want the CPU to transfer to "quick storage," is permanently stored on discs and hard drives. You can think of them as being pretty much the same thing, but the discs are small and portable, while the hard drives are large and hard to lug around.

The standard disc, also called a *floppy disc,* is a flat plastic box, about 3½" square, that houses a pancake-like disc on which information is magnetically recorded. (An older style of disc, now seen less and less, consists of a 5¼" square soft shell covering a flat, round disc.) Floppy discs are cheap, very reliable, and portable. (They can be slipped into your pocket when you go from computer to computer.) You can have your computer read information off the discs, write, erase and rewrite information over and over again.

A new type of disc, the *laser disc,* uses a laser beam to encode and read information off a flat round disc that looks and acts just like the CDs you pop into the CD player when you want to hear your favorite music. In fact, laser discs are also called *CD-ROM* discs. *ROM* stands for **R**ead **O**nly **M**emory. Laser discs can hold tremendous amounts of information, much more than regular floppy discs. Unfortunately, you can't use them to store *new* information—at least, not yet.

In order for the computer to use discs and laser discs, they have to be slid into a slot in your computer. Doing so puts them into a *disc drive* which knows how to read and write on the discs.

Like the smaller floppy discs, hard discs are essentially flat, round "pancakes" upon which information is magnetically recorded. The primary difference, practically speaking, is that the hard discs can hold much more information because they're bigger. The mechanism that surrounds them, that encodes and decodes information to and from the hard disc, is called a *hard drive.*

How fast is your hard disc?

Speed is an important measure of a hard disc's ability. The faster it spins around—*access speed*—the quicker the CPU can find information, or write in new information.

Hard disc speed is measured in *milliseconds* (*ms* for short). The lower the ms, the faster the disc. Early hard discs had ms ratings in the 60s, but today a hard disc with an ms of more than 20 is considered a "turtle."

Hard discs located in boxes sitting next to your computer are called *external hard drives*. If they're inside the computer, they're called *internal hard drives*. Information can also be stored on a *tape backup system*. Using a tape backup system is like recording all the information on your hard drives onto a large cassette tape, then playing it back when you need it. Tape backups are effective but slower than hard drives.

That's all there is to it (to begin with)

Very thick books have been written to explain the inner workings of the computer, but what you have just finished reading is, in a nutshell, how a computer works.

Knowing all of this won't make you a computer expert, but it's enough to get you started. Everything else is an elaboration of these basic concepts. Now that you know how a computer works, let's check out some tips on selecting one for yourself.

Chapter 3

Eleven tips for selecting the right computer

You probably thought that mastering computer lingo and developing a general understanding of computers and what they can do for you was the hard part. Think again. The task ahead—actually buying the machine—is often the most difficult. Some people describe it as a cross between haggling with a used car salesman and getting a tooth pulled.

With so many types of computers and peripherals available, made by many manufacturers, it can be difficult to decide which is best for you. For example, ask yourself which you should buy, Computer "A" or Computer "B":

- "A" is a 133 MHz Pentium multimedia PC with a built-in floating-point processor and 64K cache, 4 MG VRAM, 8 MG RAM expandable to 56, plus an internal 500 MG drive.

- "B" is a 486 with a math coprocessor, graphics card, quadruple-speed CD-ROM and a single-gig hard drive.

Which computer is best for you? Who knows? And you probably won't figure out which is best suited to your purposes by simply comparing their stats.

The countless different computers, screens, printers, hard drives and other devices lining the shelves can make a trip to the computer store both baffling and intimidating. There are so many things to consider: Do you want to become part of the Macintosh world or the IBM world? If it's IBM, do you want an actual IBM machine, a Packard Bell, a Compaq, a Dell or one of any number of other IBM-clones? Should you buy a black and white monitor, a color monitor, a VGA color monitor or a super VGA? Is a 500 MG hard drive enough? What about the Pentium?

The best way to begin your quest for the perfect computer is to forget about which computer you'll be buying. For now, forget about the hardware, too. Hardware is one of the last items to consider when selecting a computer.

What do people want when buying computers?

That depends on whether or not it's their first computer. According to a 1995 survey conducted by *Computer Life* magazine, 65 percent of first-time buyers rated good value for their money as their primary concern. The manufacturer's reputation was their second most important consideration.

But priorities flipped when people purchased their second computers. This time, the manufacturer's reputation was the main consideration, with multimedia capability and technical support taking second and third place.

Asking yourself the right questions

Begin the buying process by deciding what you want your computer to do, then finding the software that will do it. Only then should you look for the hardware to run that software. Long before thinking about which brand of computer or how many megs of RAM you need, ask yourself these 11 questions:

1. What are you going to use the computer for?

If you only want the computer to write reports and keep track of your checkbook, or to play some games, an inexpensive, bare-bones computer may be all that you need. But if you're going to be doing some serious number crunching, surfing the Internet in search of information, and/or handling large graphics or multimedia projects, you'll need a more extensive (and expensive) setup. Just running Windows 95 on an IBM-compatible requires significant computer power.

2. What software will you likely be using?

Now that you know what you want your computer to do, start thinking about the software you'll need to do it. This is perhaps the hardest but most vital step in deciding which computer to buy. Go to the computer laboratory at school, to a friend's house or to the computer store and try out software. Find out if you need separate word processing, graphics and database programs, or if a "combined" program such as Claris Works will work for you.

Be sure to find out what kind of software your school uses. It's best to use the same kind, if possible. If your school uses several kinds, find out which is used most in your department or among the friends or study partners you'll be working with. (You may be able to purchase the software at a discount through your school.)

3. What kind of hardware does it take to run that software?

Some software runs quite well on stripped-down, inexpensive machines. Almost any old Mac or IBM-compatible can handle basic word processing programs and smaller data bases. But other applications require more hardware power. For example:

- Microsoft's "Windows 95" requires a 386DX or higher processor, a VGA or higher-resolution graphics card and either a 3.5" high density disk drive or a CD-ROM drive. A mouse, modem, audio card and speakers are all optional.

- Microsoft's "Encarta '95" multimedia encyclopedia requires a 386SX or higher processor, a CD-ROM drive, an audio board, an SVGA 256-color monitor, a mouse and either headphones or speakers.

- Creative Multimedia's "Spanish To Go!," a Spanish language teaching program, requires a 486SX/33 or higher processor, a double-speed CD-ROM drive, a 256 color display, a SoundBlaster or compatible sound card and a microphone.

- A modem is a must for going online.

The point of this list is not to dazzle you with computer-talk, but to emphasize the importance of thinking about software *before* hardware.

Remember that although most major software is available for both Macs and IBM-compatibles, some programs are only available for one or the other.

Check the requirements *before* writing the check for your computer. (While it's already possible to buy software that will allow your Mac to read IBM discs and your IBM or clone to read Mac discs, it'll cost you.)

4. How much memory do you need to run your software?

How much RAM and hard drive memory do you expect to need now and in the near-to-medium distant future? No one can predict what you'll need two years from now, but you can plan ahead by thinking about programs you'll be using, then checking their requirements. For example:

- System software "Windows 95" requires a minimum of 4 MG RAM (but 8 MG are recommended), with at least 45 MG of available hard drive space.

- Microsoft's "Word For Windows 95," another popular word processing program, requires at least 6 MG RAM. As for hard drive space, at least 8 MG are required for the "compact" setup, 16 MG for the "typical" setup and 35 MG for the "custom" version.

- Running "Your Personal Trainer for the SAT" by Davidson on a Mac or in a Windows environment requires at least 4 MG of RAM.

- "Dr. Ruth's Encyclopedia of Sex" (CD-ROM for Windows) requires 4 MG of RAM and 5 MG of available hard drive space.

Think about which programs you'll be using *before* you lock yourself in by purchasing a computer with inadequate memory. You can add memory to some computers after you buy them, but it costs extra. And you may not be able to add enough, no matter what you're willing to spend.

5. What kind of hardware does your school use?

If your school uses the Mac, it makes sense for you to buy a Mac rather than an IBM-compatible, and vice versa. Purchasing equipment that's identical or similar to that used at school makes your life simpler.

6. *Where will you be using the computer?*

Will you be putting the computer on a large, specially built desk in a spacious study, or setting it on a rickety little table in a crowded dormitory room? If you have a lot of room, you can handle a more expansive setup. If not, you'll have to look for something more compact.

And if you'll be using the computer in multiple locations (at home, in the library and on airplanes), a laptop may make more sense.

7. *How are you going to protect your files?*

Do you intend to copy sensitive files that you can't afford to lose on extra discs? On a separate hard drive? Or is a tape backup system more appropriate for you? The answer depends on how many "I can't afford to lose them" files you'll be creating, how long they are and how often you'll be working with them.

If you're simply writing short papers and keeping a simple database on your computer, you can easily back up the data on 3.5" discs. But if you have more complex files, and you access them often, a tape backup system will make it easier for you to protect your work.

Apple versus Big Blue

Somewhere in your decision-making process, you'll come up against the Macintosh versus IBM-compatible (also known as the Mac versus DOS) question.

Comparing the Mac and IBM-compatible can be like discussing religion or politics—many people refuse to even consider the possibility that the other kind of computer has any merit. The truth? Neither one is inherently better or worse. Both systems have pluses and minuses. Figure out which one gives *you* the most pluses and fewest minuses. Here's a quick comparison:

Usability. The Mac is easier to learn and use. The IBM-compatible world is closing the gap with Windows 95, but still lags behind.

Cost. With many manufacturers vying for the computer buyer's dollar, IBM-compatibles cost less than the Mac. Newly introduced Mac clones are expected to bring the cost of the Mac down.

Software. Much more software is written for IBM-compatibles than for the Mac, but plenty of software, including most major word processing, spreadsheet and database programs, are available for the Mac. And newer versions of many programs written for Windows are almost identical to their Mac counterparts, which means you can easily go from one type of computer to the other.

Cross compatibility. The newer Macs and IBM-compatibles are capable of reading files written for either type of computer.

Availability. It's easier to find IBM-compatible computers and software since more are available.

Future fear. Some industry analysts suggest that Apple, the maker of the Mac, may not survive as an independent company, and that Mac users will have no place to turn to for service. No one really knows which companies will be around in the future. Some seemingly prosperous companies have gone bankrupt, while troubled companies have weathered difficult financial storms. Even if Apple were to run into trouble, it would most likely be bought out by or merged with another computer company that would continue to make Macs. With millions of Macs in use, even if Apple does vanish, independent shops will undoubtedly continue to service them.

Once you've narrowed down your choices, you can then consider these questions:

8. How much can you afford to spend?

With all their high-tech gizmos, computers are very enticing, but your infatuation with the little machine can quickly translate into serious dinero. It's remarkably easy to convince yourself you simply *must* have that quad-speed CD-ROM drive or that super-fast color printer. And computer salespeople will be more than happy to show you the exciting, costly extras. That's why it's best to decide how much you can afford to spend *before* you go shopping—and stick to your budget!

Although prices vary greatly from store to store and sale to sale, you can expect to spend anywhere from $1,200 to $3,000 for a personal computer. Don't forget to include the cost of software in your budget. The software you need can cost anywhere from a couple hundred dollars on up—way up.

9. Will you pay more for a recognizable brand name, or do you want to save money with a lesser-known company?

Buying an IBM will cost more than an almost identical clone made by Dell or Compaq. But some people prefer to go with known manufacturers that have a long and strong record of customer service.

10. How much time do you want to spend setting up and configuring your computer?

You can design the "perfect" computer system for yourself by mixing and matching components from various manufacturers. But if you purchase a CPU from one company, an external hard drive from another, a monitor from a third and a printer and tape backup system from yet another, you may spend quite a bit of time trying to make all the pieces fit together. On the other hand, an "all in one" system made by a single manufacturer will probably require relatively little time and effort to assemble and put into operating order, especially if it comes with software pre-installed.

The Mac is the leader in the "plug and play" area. Its hardware is easy to set up, and you don't have to configure your computer when installing new software.

11. Does the manufacturer of the computer you're considering offer service and support?

If you have a question, does the company provide a toll-free number to call for help? Do they offer that help at no cost, or do you have to pay? What about the warranty? And if your computer breaks, can you take it to the local computer fix-it shop, or do you have to mail it to Alaska to be serviced?

Determining what you must have

Asking yourself the right questions, and seriously considering the answers, can save you a lot of grief, time and money. Using the form provided, jot down your answers to these key questions *before* going to the computer store.

1. What are you going to use the computer for?

_____

_____

_____

_____

_____

_____

2. What software will you likely be using?

Word processing	Graphics
Spreadsheet	Multimedia
Database	Games
Desktop publishing	Other

Which software in particular?

_____

_____

_____

_____

_____

And what software does your school use?

_____

_____

3. What kind of hardware does it take to run that software?

_____

_____

_____

Go to the computer store and get information off the boxes for each of the three most important programs you'll be using. (Photocopy and fill out the form on page 40.)

Put it all together by selecting the most common requirements in each category. (Obviously, you can't decide you need a Mac because you've selected three software programs for the Mac and only two for the IBM. You'll have to select either a Mac or an IBM-type of computer. Remember, however, that newer machines can "read" files from both types of machines, and, with the right enhancements, can run many of each other's programs.)

Program:

Name of program _____

Type of computer needed:

❑ Mac

❑ IBM-compatible

❑ Other _____

Processor (386, 486, etc.): _____

Operating system:

❑ DOS version: _____

❑ Windows version: _____

❑ Mac system: _____

❑ Other: _____

Disk drive: ❑ 3.5" ❑ 5.25" ❑ CD-ROM

Monitor: ❑ Black & White ❑ Color ❑ VGA ❑ SVGA

Number of colors required: _____

Mouse or pointing device: _____

Sound board: _____

Headphones/speakers: _____

Modem: _____ Baud rate: _____

Printer: _____

Networking capabilities: _____

Other: _____

_____

_____

4. How much memory do you need to run your software?

Remember that some programs function with a minimum amount of RAM and hard drive space, but do much better with more memory.

Program #1:

Name of program _____

Minimum RAM required _____

RAM recommended _____

Minimum available hard drive space required _____

Available hard drive space recommended _____

Program #2:

Name of program _____

Minimum RAM required _____

RAM recommended _____

Minimum available hard drive space required _____

Available hard drive space recommended _____

Program #3:

Name of program _____

Minimum RAM required _____

RAM recommended _____

Minimum available hard drive space required _____

Available hard drive space recommended _____

Look through the requirements for the three programs above, then write down the greatest numbers below:

RAM required _____

RAM recommended _____

Available hard drive space required _____

Available hard drive space recommended _____

5. What kind of hardware does your school use?

Computer: _____

System: _____

6. *Where will you be using the computer?*

Describe the places where the computer will be used. How much space is available? Will you be moving the computer around?

_____

_____

_____

_____

7. *How are you going to protect your files?*
   - ❑ By backing them up on floppy discs.
   - ❑ By backing them up on another hard drive.
   - ❑ With a tape backup system.
   - ❑ By e-mailing them to a friend.

8. *How much can you afford to spend?*

I can spend an absolute maximum of $_____

9. *Will you pay more for a recognizable brand name, or do you prefer to save money with a lesser-known company?*
   - ❑ I prefer the security of a well-known brand name computer.
   - ❑ I'm willing to take a chance with a lesser-known company.

10. *How much time are you willing to spend setting up and configuring your computer?*
   - ❑ As long as it takes.
   - ❑ Many hours.
   - ❑ A few hours, tops.
   - ❑ As little as possible.

11. Does the manufacturer of the computer you're considering offer service and support?

Manufacturer #1:

Describe warranty on hardware: _____

Describe the support they offer:

❑ None.

❑ You pay for the phone call and the support.

❑ You pay for the call but the support is free.

❑ Both the call and the support are free.

❑ The support is limited to _____ hours or _____ calls.

❑ The support is unlimited.

Manufacturer #2:

Describe warranty on hardware: _____

Describe the support they offer:

❑ None.

❑ You pay for the phone call and the support.

❑ You pay for the call but the support is free.

❑ Both the call and the support are free.

❑ The support is limited to _____ hours or _____ calls.

❑ The support is unlimited.

Manufacturer #3:

Describe warranty on hardware: _____

Describe the support they offer:

❑ None.

❑ You pay for the phone call and the support.

❑ You pay for the call but the support is free.

❑ Both the call and the support are free.

❑ The support is limited to _____ hours or _____ calls.

❑ The support is unlimited.

And what you'd really, really like

Now that you've answered these questions to help you decide what you absolutely *must* have, you can think about what you'd *like* to have. For example:

- You might only *need* a dot matrix printer, but a laser printer will make your reports and graphics look better.

- A slow printer is fine if you don't print very often, but a faster one may be necessary if you have to print out hard copies often.

- A small monitor is adequate for most purposes, but if you're doing a lot of desktop publishing, a screen that shows the entire page is better. And if you're using spreadsheets a lot, an extra wide screen will be helpful.

- A color screen with 256 colors is more than enough for most applications, but if you're studying art or graphic arts, you may need more.

On a separate sheet of paper, describe the extra features that will be helpful to you, and why.

Wishing on a star

Now that you know what you must have, and what would be helpful to add, you can prepare your "wish list."

Type of computer:
❑ Mac ❑ IBM-compatible ❑ Other _____
Processor (386, 486, etc.): _____
Operating System: ❑ DOS version: _____
❑ Windows version: _____
❑ Mac system: _____
❑ Other: _____

RAM: _____

Hard drive size: _____

Disk Drive: ❑ 3.5" ❑ 5.25" ❑ CD-ROM

Monitor: ❑ Black & White ❑ Color ❑ VGA ❑ SVGA

Number of colors required: _____

Screen size: _____

Mouse or pointing device: _____

Sound board: _____

Headphones/Speakers: _____

Modem: _____ Baud Rate: _____

Printer: _____

Networking capabilities: _____

Printer: _____Type: _____

Black & White or Color: _____

Pages per minute: _____

Keyboard: _____

Other: _____

_____

_____

And I want it all for *no more* than $_____

This is not an all-inclusive list, and it does not address all the ins and outs of computers, monitors, printers and other hardware. But it does narrow the field considerably, making your final selection much easier.

Now you have to "go out into the field." Visit the local computer stores and call the mail-order computer stores. Tell them exactly what you want, and have them give you a quote—in writing. Make sure that every little thing is included in the quote; you don't want any surprises later. For each store, note the following:

Use Your Computer

Name of store: _____

Salesperson: _____

Date: _____

My budget: $_____

Price quote: $_____

This store offers support: ❏ Yes ❏ No

This store has a repair department: ❏ Yes ❏ No

The store has a good reputation: ❏ Yes ❏ No

Extras they're offering me: _____

Some final tips before you buy

- Shop around. You'll find computers in computer stores, computer "super" stores, electronic stores, department stores and large discount warehouses.

- Get written quotes, and make sure that everything you want is included in the quote.

- Don't be afraid to haggle. Prices are rarely fixed, and you can often negotiate a better deal.

- Find out if the computer you want is in stock, or if you have to wait for delivery.

- Ask whether or not the store stands behind what they sell, or if you have to go to the manufacturer in case of a problem.

- Tell the salesperson that you want your system software and other key programs pre-installed by the store—especially if you're a computer novice.

- Be prepared to go elsewhere if the salespeople don't answer all your questions. If they aren't terribly helpful *before* they have your money, how helpful will they be once they have it?

At last! You've bought your computer! Congratulations!

Chapter 4

Software that teaches

Software is the key to computers; without it, all of that expensive hardware can't do anything.

The programs (software) that you purchase and plug into your hardware are really just directions to the computer which have been placed on a disc or laser disc. They're nothing more than "instruction books" written in code that the computer can understand.

Ah, but what those instruction books can make a computer do! They can fill your screen with the complete works of many authors, along with pictures and commentary. They can ask you hundreds of questions, then give you the answers, to help you prepare for tests such as the SAT or GRE. They can "speak" to you in French or many other foreign languages so that you can hear how the language is supposed to sound. They can take you on tours of foreign countries, lands under the seas, battlefields and the inner workings of the human body. They can play music, show you great artwork and recite poetry. They can, in short, be superb educational assistants.

In this chapter, we'll look at some of the educational software available today. The software reviewed is not necessarily the "best" software; instead it's a sampling of what's out there, a look at the many computerized teaching aids that can help you increase your knowledge, pass a test or class or just have fun learning.

Before you buy

When deciding whether to buy educational software, remember that:

- There is no such thing as the "best" program in any educational category. Some are stuffed with complex information, while others focus on a few simplified concepts. Some rely heavily on text, while others delight you with sounds, pictures, videos and games. Some are geared for younger students, while others are for the more advanced. Some are plain looking and bare-bones, others high tech and glitzy. Which one is best? The one that best serves *your* needs.

- You can find much of this same information on the Internet or through the online services, and information on a computer disc can quickly become dated. However, there's nothing like having what you need, right at hand, when you need it. And you only have to pay for information on a disc once, when you buy the program. (There are ongoing charges for using the Internet and online services.)

- Your school may already have software you like in the classrooms or computer laboratory. See what your school has to offer before buying your own.

- It's best not to rely solely on the advertising copy you read on the software boxes. Talk with your friends and read software reviews before parting with your money. You can also contact the software manufacturer and request a demo disc, if they have one.
- You must check the side of the software box for hardware requirements to make sure your computer can run the software. Be wary of "minimum" and "suggested" RAM requirements. "Minimum" means just that—you'll get minimal performance from the software if you have the minimum RAM. It's better to have the "suggested" RAM. (In most cases, the suggestion is really a requirement.)

A few organizational notes

For the sake of convenience, I've divided the reviews into anatomy, art, astronomy, college, geography, grammar, health, history, hobbies, language, literature, mathematics, music, nature & natural history, physics, places & peoples, reference works, religion and science.

The first item in parenthesis tells whether the program requires the Macintosh (Mac), DOS and/or Windows (Win) system.

The manufacturer is listed next. If you have any questions about the program, or want to know how to go about purchasing it, look for the manufacturer's number in the Appendix.

Finally, the actual price you pay for the product depends on whether you purchase it at a computer store, a "warehouse" or "club" store or through the mail, but I've listed the approximate cost here.

With all that in mind, let's take a look at some of the many educational and reference programs available on the market today.

Anatomy: *Virtual Body* (Win, IVI Publishing, $20-25). Detailed multimedia look at the human body. Investigation of body systems, experiments and lab tasks. Select from a battery of questions, then explore the answers.

A.D.A.M. Standard-Student Edition (Mac/Win, A.D.A.M. Software, $135-150). Work through "layers" of drawings as you delve into the workings of the organs, immune system, digestive system, etc. See drawings from different perspectives, perform "surgery" on diagrams.

Art: *Matisse, Aragon, Prokofiev* (Mac/Win, New Line New Media, $45-50). Matisse's paintings, Aragon's poems and Prokofiev's music with text that explains the relationship between the artists and their time.

A Passion for Art (Mac/Win, Corbis Publishing, $40). More than 300 paintings by Picasso, Cezanne and others, and a time line covering the years 1830 to 1940.

Microsoft Art Gallery allows you to see 2,000 pieces from the National Gallery in London; *Poetry in Motion* presents 24 modern poets through sound and picture. You might also want to check out *Tate Gallery: Exploring Modern Art* (Attica Cybernetics) and *Monet, Verlaine, Debussy: The Impressionist Revolution* (New Line Cinema).

Astronomy: *RedShift Multimedia Astronomy* (Mac/Win, Maris Multimedia, $40-50). Information from American and Soviet space programs. Using star chart simulations, predict future location of heavenly bodies. More than 700 photos, video clips, "tours" of lunar eclipses, other stellar events and more than 200,000 stars.

Venus Explorer (Mac/DOS, $70). With images based on information produced by NASA's Magellan probe, see the planet's mountains, chasms, craters and other features.

College: *SAT I* (Mac/Win, Cliffs Notes, $45-50). Begins with a diagnostic exam, then presents student with personal study plan. Hundreds of questions to work your way through math, analogies, reading and sentence completion. Comes with *SAT I Preparation Guide.*

Your Personal Trainer for the SAT (Mac/Win, Davidson, $35). Combines practice tests with assessments. Five sample tests, two printed tests. Question-answer format teaches reading, vocabulary, analogy, algebra and geometry skills. Choose difficulty level and ask for analysis as you go. Prints 250 vocabulary words on cards. College Comparison Graph compares your scores to those of freshmen at some 300 schools.

Your Personal Trainer for the GRE (Mac/Win, Davidson, $35). After taking pre-test to detect strengths and weaknesses, students can review test-taking strategies, then work through practice sessions to improve verbal, analytical and mathematical skills.

On Campus 96 (Mac/Win, Kaplan Educational Center, $40-50). Text, narration, video and maps present more than 1,700 universities and colleges. Includes rankings, requirements, majors, athletics, activities, costs, career and financial aid information and a standardized application accepted at many colleges.

U.S. News and World Report's Getting Into College, 1996 Edition (Win, Creative Multimedia). 1,400 colleges/universities. Suggests schools after you enter preferences. Looks at financial aid, studying abroad, dorm and college life, admission tests, interviews, getting recommendations, related articles, names/addresses of various organizations.

Cash for Class (Win, Redheads Software, $35-40). Type in personal profile, including achievements, ethnic and religious background, interests, etc. Compiles list of scholarships for which you may be eligible and tells you how to apply. Prints letters of interest and mailing labels.

Geography: *3D Atlas* (Mac/Win, ABC/EA Home Software, $80). Political, topographical, atmospheric, environmental and other points of view. Includes cultural, political, economic and other information, pictures and video presentations of peoples of the world, "flights" over the landscape and a game.

National Geographic's Picture Atlas of The World (Mac/Win, National Geographic Society, $50-60). Native music, samples of the language, videos and other enhancements. General, historical, statistical and political information on various countries.

Global Explorer (Win, IVI Publishing, $60). Many highly detailed maps and information on every country's geography, population, government, wildlife and military.

Grammar: *Grammatik* (Mac/Win, Novell Inc., $40-50). Corrects grammar, allows you to set degree of "correctness," rates prose for readability, vocabulary and complexity.

Health: *Dr. Ruth's Encyclopedia of Sex* (Win, Creative Multimedia, $30). Biological, psychological, religious, health, cultural and legal aspects of sex. Dr. Ruth Westheimer's image and voice, interactive anatomy chart, quiz, 200 questions and answers. Radio show excerpts, video clips and animations teach, for example, how to perform self exams.

History: *Compton's Encyclopedia of American History* (Win, Compton's NewMedia, $35-40). Sound, video clips, pictures, definitions, profiles and related articles.

Ancient Lands (Win, Microsoft Corp., $30-40). Through text and pictures, visit Egypt, Rome, Greece and Atlantis.

Our Times Multimedia Encyclopedia of the 20th Century (Win, Vicarious Inc., $70). Explore by topic or keyword, switching to video clips or essays describing themes and thoughts that shaped our world and ourselves. More than 52,000 articles, 2,500 images, maps and graphs, two hours of narration, catalogs of cultural, sports, political and other events and an enormous number of links.

Normandy: The Great Crusade (Win, The Discovery Channel, $35-40). Award-winning program blends photos, sound clips, film, maps and text. Allows you to choose how you will learn.

Ideas That Changed the World (Win, Cambrix Publishing, $45-50). Looks at the thinkers and the results of their ideas, from early times to the present. Text, illustrations, timelines, games and indexes.

Her Heritage (Win, Cambrix Publishing, $30). Over 1,000 women who have shaped the nation, from Betsy Ross to Supreme Court Justice Sandra Day O'Connor, described in words, pictures and video clips.

Smithsonian's America: An Interactive Exhibition of American History and Culture (Win, Creative Multimedia, $30). Some 1,000 historical artifacts, documents, photos, newsreels, audio and video clips. American ideals and images, entertainers, politics, the Western frontier, time and space, home life.

Hobbies: The *Encyclopedia of U.S. Postage Stamps* (Mac/Win, Zane Publishing, $25). Photos and histories of more than 2,000 postage stamps by subject matter, series, date or key word.

Garden Encyclopedia (Win, Books That Work, $30). Common and scientific names of plants, diseases, pests, etc.

The *Complete Baseball Guide 1995 Edition* (Win, Microsoft, $30-40). Stats on every player who ever played in the big leagues, more than 2,000 biographies and pictures and audio/video clips of great moments.

Comic Book Confidential (Mac, $50). Mixes comic book history with film clips of the Congressional investigation into this art form in the 1950s, text, interviews, animation and photographs. Follows the comic through its "Golden Era" to modern times.

Language: *Learn to Speak Spanish* (Mac/Win, The Learning Company, $90-100). Lessons in Spanish with short videos, music and pictures, dealing with everyday terms a traveler needs to master. Listen to native speakers, then pronounce the words yourself. Includes workbook.

Power Spanish (Win, Bayware, Inc., $85-95). Focuses on similarities between Spanish and English. Video clips, games and helpful hints appear as you work. Adjustable pronunciation speed. Comes with *Spanish Assistant* program, which translates documents.

You might also want to investigate *Learn To Speak French* and other language programs by HyperGlost Software, and Transparent Language's *Now!* series (*French Now!, Italian Now!, Russian Now!*, etc.).

Literature: *The Complete Works of Shakespeare* (Andromedia Interactive), *The Crucible* (Penguin Electronic Publishing), *Trouble Is My Business: The Raymond Chandler Library* and *The Essential Frankenstein* (Byron Priess Multimedia), *Of Mice and Men* and others (Byron Priess Multimedia's John Steinbeck Library).

Grolier Science Fiction—The Multimedia Encyclopedia of Science Fiction (Mac/Win, Grolier Electronic Publishing, $50-60). Includes 4,500 entries covering 400 years, interactive features, movie clips and photos.

Mathematics: *World Math Challenge Volume 1* (Win, Pacific Software, $45). Pits you against Japanese students taking junior high placement exams. Using questions from the test, select difficulty level. Ask for hints or explanations as you go. Questions go up to pre-algebra level.

Alge-Blaster 3. (Mac/Win, Davidson, $35). Designed for junior high and high school students, uses games to teach 27 algebraic topics including word problems, graphing, radicals, slopes and points, factors and other subjects covered in first-year algebra.

Music: *Beethoven and Beyond* (Mac/Win, The Voyager Company, $25). Essays on Beethoven, Mozart, Brahms and other classical composers mixed with pictures and sound clips.

Jazz: A Multimedia History (Win, Compton's NewMedia, $30). Lengthy text, photographs, video clips and recreations of key jazz selections.

Musical Instruments (Mac, Microsoft Corp., $35). Look at, listen to and read the history of every instrument imaginable, from accordion to zither. Explore musical instruments randomly, by country, origin, "family" or use.

History of Music: The Collection (Mac/Win, ZCI Publishing, $30). Examines Western music from the Classical era through rock and roll, the relationships between musical styles and between music and culture.

There are numerous other music education and appreciation programs, including *The Multimedia Mozart, The Multimedia Beethoven, The Multimedia Strauss* and *The Multimedia Stravinsky*, all by Microsoft Corp.

Nature & natural history: *In the Company of Whales* (Win, The Discovery Channel, $35). Comprehensive look at humpbacks, grays and others. Narrated videos, text, pictures and commonly asked questions.

The Animals! (Win, DOS, The Software Toolworks, $100-120). Tour of the San Diego Zoo. Voluminous text with more than 1,000 photographs, video and audio clips.

Ocean Planet Smithsonian (Mac/Win, The Discovery Channel, $50). Text and video describe everything from plankton to whales, from currents to the Gulf Stream. Resources for further study.

Physics: *The Ultimate Einstein* (Mac/Win, Byron Preiss Multimedia, $50). Actor portraying the great physicist discusses science, religion, the arms race and other topics. Animated sequences demonstrate relativity, black holes, etc. Includes texts of two books written by Einstein and other materials.

A Brief History of Time (Win, Blasterware, $55-65). Multimedia presentation of Stephen Hawking's book of the same name. Animation and pictures help illustrate points as you read or have the computer read aloud.

Places & peoples: *Explore the Grand Canyon* (Win, Media Terra/The Coriolis Group, $50). Extensive text, over 3,000 photos, maps, video clips and time-lapse film give you the feeling that you're in the canyon. Geological formations, wildlife, plants and more. Visit campsites of explorers, learning what it was like for them through excerpts from their writings.

The First Emperor of China (Mac/Win, $50). Takes you to the tomb of Qin Shi Huang Di, the kingdom's first emperor. Text, sound and images bring the ancient treasures of the Emperor alive. Includes audio guide to pronouncing Chinese words, glossary and bibliography.

Passage to Vietnam (Mac/Win, Against All Odds Productions, $60). The people and their country. Set to music, "look in" on a traditional Vietnamese wedding, explore a Buddhist temple, visit a workplace and more.

Reference works: *Bookshelf '95* (Mac/Win, Microsoft Corp., $40-50). *American Heritage Dictionary, Roget's Thesaurus, Columbia Dictionary of Quotations, Concise Columbia Encyclopedia, Hammond World Atlas, The People's Chronology, World Almanac and Book of Facts 1995* and *National ZIP Code and Post Office Directory* on one CD. Several hundred video and audio clips, and spoken pronunciations of some 80,000 words.

The 1996 Grolier Multimedia Encyclopedia (Mac/Win, Grolier Electronic Publishing, $50-60). More than 33,000 articles, 900 maps, 8,000 enlargeable images, 150 documents, music, timelines, a yearbook of news between January 1994 and June 1995. Clicking on a picture of a lion causes the lion's skin to disappear, revealing organs inside the body (which are labeled). Video clips of people who have shaped the world. Can be linked to CompuServe, allowing you to switch to corresponding sections online.

Encyclopaedia Britannica CD 2.0 (Mac/Win, Encyclopaedia Britannica Inc., $450-500). Very comprehensive and text-intensive. Few interactive features. Search by topic, or type a question such as "How does the heart beat?"

Merriam-Webster's Collegiate Dictionary (Mac/Win, Merriam-Webster Electronic Publishing, $45-50). Contains more than 200,000 definitions, with information on proper usage, pronunciation, history, synonyms, rhymes, words that sound the same but are spelled differently, illustrations, word puzzles and more.

You might also investigate Future Vision Multimedia's *Infopedia* and Microsoft's *Encarta*.

Religion: *The New Family Bible: From the Garden to the Promised Land* (Mac/DOS, Time Warner Interactive, $30). Read and watch 40 different Bible stories. When you come across a difficult word, have the computer pronounce it. Maps of events and family trees.

Verse Search 6.0 (Mac/Win/DOS, Bible Research Systems, $150). *Not* a multimedia tour of the Bible. Designed for serious study, it allows you to rapidly search through the Bible by keyword. Maps and other information.

Pathways Through Jerusalem (FutureVision), *Compton's Multimedia Bible* and *The Dead Sea Scrolls* (Logos) are others.

Science: *The Way Things Work* (Mac/Win, DK Multimedia, $45-55). Multimedia exploration of science, inventors and machines, emphasizing practical "hows" and "whys" of many items and principles we use. Look at individual machines and read biographies of inventors.

...and much more

The software reviewed in this chapter is just a small sampling of the computerized teaching aids you can buy. Talk to friends, read computer magazines and check out computer stores to find the educational software that's best for you.

Chapter 5

Going online

Going online is easy, right? You just have to master a few concepts and techniques, and learn the difference between the *Information Superhighway, the Internet, Mosaic, Gopher, the Web, WAIS, BBSes, servers, browsers, online services* and *ISPs*. It's so simple that any 10-year-old can do it. In fact, many adults turn to 10-year-olds to explain it all to them, and still can't quite figure it out.

That's a shame, because going online puts a tremendous amount of information at your fingertips. Going online is especially helpful to students, for it gives them access to a mind-boggling array of educational and research facilities, including:

- Hundreds of journals and magazines.
- Newspapers from around the country.
- Encyclopedias.
- Bulletin boards.

Use Your Computer

- Homework Helper, Cognito and similar "answer finders."
- Online "teachers" who personally answer questions.
- Internet access to information sites filled with documents, statistics, lists and bibliographies on such subjects as abortion, affirmative action, animal rights, art, astronomy, aviation, biology, business/economics, chemistry, civil liberties, computers, criminology, food, dance, demography, domestic violence, feminism, film, genealogy, genetics, government, health, history, human rights, international affairs, literature, magic, mathematics, military, physics, places at home and abroad, politics, religion, space, theater, weather—and just about anything else you can think of.
- Mini-courses in math, English, physics, American history and most other subjects.
- Information about the SAT, GRE and other tests, plus practice tests.
- Information about hundreds of colleges, their admission requirements, student demographics and costs.
- Information on financial aid.
- An opportunity to "chat" with other students.
- The ability to contact experts in every field, many of whom will take the time to answer questions or engage in debates.

...and much, much more. New online features make it possible for you to request information on any subject. Think of all the time and effort you'll save!

Before you begin surfing

Fortunately, you don't have to be a 10-year-old to understand the information superhighway. Adults can get into the driver's seat and begin cruising, too, with just a little study. Let's begin by reviewing some basic concepts.

Going online simply means hooking your computer up to another computer—or to many others. You can go online by:

- Physically running a cable between your computer and someone else's. (A business will often connect its computers with cables, putting them all online with each other).

- Connecting computers via the telephone. If you connect over the phone wires, you'll need a *modem* to convert the computers' signals into a form that can travel through the phone system.

That's it, that's all that "going online" means: Allowing computers to communicate with each other. You've "lined up" your computer with another so that the information can flow.

Once online, you can begin cruising the *Information Superhighway*, also known as the Global Information Highway, the Information Highway, the info highway, The Highway and cyberspace.

The information superhighway is a rather nebulous term because the highway is not a physical structure, like the interstate highway system that crisscrosses the country. But it *is* a lot like those highways in that it gets you where you want to go. Instead of taking you from city to city, however, the information superhighway takes you from information site to information site. Harvard and the

Louvre Museum are information sites on the superhighway. So are the White House, NASA and many city and state government offices.

I said that the information superhighway takes you from one information site to another to emphasize that the highway *itself* is not important. It's the information available at different points along the highway that matters. Think of the superhighway as the roadway, and the information stops as cities, towns, parks, monuments, mountains, oceans, lakes, deserts and beaches that you may want to visit.

Obviously, you don't physically "go" anywhere on the info highway. Instead, your computer reaches out and retrieves the information for you. Suppose you want to get information from a book that's in the Library of Congress in Washington, D.C. Instead of getting into your car and driving to the nation's capital, you simply instruct your computer to "go" into the Library's computer via the superhighway, and bring back the info.

What kind of information is on the information superhighway? Almost everything. Universities and research centers are online. So are federal, state and local governments, libraries, planetariums, newspapers, magazines, museums, political parties, sports teams, gardening clubs and Grateful Dead fan clubs, just to mention a few.

The amount of information on the superhighway is literally limitless, because you can use the highway to "speak" to millions of other people via computer. Countless experts and amateurs in all fields are online, and many will allow you to take information out of their computers, or will answer your questions.

Of course, there are no free lunches. You may have to pay for access to these services, or your school may pay for you. Either way, there's often a charge.

The "main drag"

We drive our vehicles on all kinds of roads: interstate highways, freeways, boulevards, cul-de-sacs, mountain roads—even off-road. Likewise, the information highway has main roads and side streets. Some are well-lit and easy to follow, while others are blind alleys.

The main "road" on the information superhighway is the *Internet*. But there are many other, smaller "roads" on the highway. Three students who "talk" to each other via computer and share information for their English essays are part of the highway. But they're way off the main road.

The Internet, the main road, is really an international network of computer networks, with no boundaries or limits. Most anyone can set him- or herself up as an information site on the Internet, or can cruise from site to site. All he or she needs is the right computer equipment.

Originally called ARPAnet, the Internet officially began back in the 1960s when the United States Department of Defense decided to hook together (network) certain computers. The idea was simply to make it easier to transfer defense information from one computer to another in case one of them broke. Soon, computers from NASA, universities and research centers hooked up to this network, and the Internet was born. For many years, the Internet was only used by researchers, scientists and the government, primarily because relatively few people had computers and there was little information on the Internet that was of interest to the average citizen.

This started to change in the 1980s when computers became smaller and more affordable. More people went online, cruising around the Internet and other parts of the information highway. Unfortunately, traveling the Internet was difficult, for there were few good "maps" to guide you, few standard "signs" to tell you where you were or what to do. You had to know a lot about various computers and computer "styles" in order to navigate from one info site to the next. And there were no "telephone books" or directories telling you what information sites existed or where they were. For the average person, prying information out of the Internet was like trying to find a little store by wandering through dark and twisty alleyways in an unfamiliar part of town, where there were no street signs, no address numbers and no signs in the store windows.

To make matters even more confusing, not every information site on the info highway was actually *on* the Internet. Many were *bulletin board systems,* also known as bulletin boards and BBSes. BBSes are like little roads, off the beaten track, that take you to one information site only. A bulletin board information site is often a single computer in someone's home that houses information on a single subject, or simply acts as a "message board" where people can post information or leave questions on a certain subject. (No one knows how many BBSes there are today. Most estimates place the number somewhere between 50,000 and 100,000.)

In other words, there was information galore, but it was hard to get. With the road so bumpy and poorly lit, most of us easily got lost.

Road maps

Fortunately, many "road maps" to the Internet and other parts of the information highway have been developed, making it easy for even a computer novice to zip from information site to site. For example, the *World Wide Web,* also known as the *web* or *WWW,* was developed as a navigational "map" of the Internet, helping people find what they were looking for. Other programs, such as *Mosaic* and *Netscape,* also help you *browse* (search) the Net.

Going on your own

Linking up to the Internet is easy. You simply go on-line through an *Internet Service Provider (ISP)*, a company that puts your computer in touch with the others (for a fee). Students may be able to tap into the Internet via their school computers, and some businesses provide the same service to their employees. Some local bulletin board systems allow you to tap into the Internet and, in some areas, you can get on the main road of the information highway via a "freenet" (for free).

Private/public roads

You can also plug into the Internet by way of commercial (for-profit) *online services* such as America Online, CompuServe, Prodigy, GEnie, eWorld and Delphi.

These online services are part of the information highway. But instead of putting you on the public highways of the Internet, these online services provide you with a combination of "private" and "public" roads. They allow you access to a large number of information sites, many of which can only be reached through *them*. In other words, you can only get to these "private" information sites by way of "private toll roads" owned by one online service or the other. If, for example, *ABC Encyclopedia* has signed an exclusive contract with America Online, then you can only "get to" *ABC Encyclopedia* by signing up with America Online.

E-mail

One of the most popular online activities is sending *e-mail* (electronic mail). In order to send and receive e-mail, you need an e-mail address. Some typical (and real) e-mail addresses are:

president@whitehouse.gov
(to leave a message for the President of the United States)

femsuprem-request@resaissoft.com
(to get on the mailing list for a discussion group called FemSuprem)

letters@news.latimes.com
(to send a letter to the editor of the *Los Angeles Times*)

letters@newsweek.com
(to send a letter to the editor of *Newsweek*)

wsmith@wordsmith.org
(to receive "A Word A Day" via e-mail)

Deciphering e-mail addresses

The mysterious codes which are used as addresses on the online services are easy to decipher if you understand the system. They can be broken down into three parts: the user's name, the computer/location and the domain.

1. User name

For most of us, the important part of an address is the *user name,* which comes first. The user name is the name used by the person, group or company that "lives" at that address. User names can be made up of various combinations of characters. For example: "KristenB" (for Kristen Buie), "BBFC" (for a Beach Boys fan club), "gccpr" (for the Giant Computer Company's Public Relations Department).

Some user names are full names or abbreviations. Others are fanciful, such as "Great1," "2Cool," "Doc2B" or "6Smiths." Some online services, such as CompuServe, issue all-numeric user names.

2. Computer/location

Next comes the name of the computer and/or location (also known as the host name). For example:

"@aol" means "at America Online."

"@eWorld" means "at eWorld" (Apple Computer's online service).

"@WHITEHOUSE" means "at the White House."

3. The domain

Finally, the three-letter abbreviation at the end of each address indicates the domain. Six domains are used in the United States:

"com" for commercial services.
"edu" for educational institutions.
"gov" for the government.
"mil" for the military.
"net" for an Internet provider.
"org" for an organization.

Other countries have their own domains and abbreviations, such as "au" for Australia and "ca" for Canada.

Putting it all together

From right to left, an e-mail address describes ever-larger entities. First is the individual user, then the specific computer, then perhaps a larger network to which the computer belongs, then the domain.

The "@" in an e-mail address is pronounced "at," while a period (".") is pronounced "dot." This means that "VICE PRESIDENT@WHITEHOUSE.COM is pronounced as "vice president at whitehouse dot com."

A quick look at some online services

Millions of people have signed up with commercial on-line services. Although limited, these "package tours" are generally easy to use and offer a variety of other services, including news, educational information, financial information, entertainment and shopping.

Let's take a brief look at America Online and Prodigy, two of the "big three" online services, plus eWorld, GEnie and the AT&T Business Network. In Chapter 6 we will delve deeper into ways that students can use America Online for education and research.

America Online

A popular service with over three million subscribers, America Online is commonly referred to AOL. It has separate sections called Today's News, Personal Finance, Clubs & Interests, Computing, Travel, Marketplace, People Connection, Newsstand, Entertainment, Education, Reference Desk, Internet Connection, Sports and Kids Only.

Today's News. Presents the news, with separate sections for national and international news, business, sports, etc. A "Search News" feature allows you to call up just the topic or story you want.

Personal Finance. Includes a *Nightly Business Report*, *Business Week Online*, the *Fidelity Online Investor Center*, information about various companies, stock quotes, magazines such as *Consumer Reports* and *Inc. Magazine Online*, and other business-related items.

Clubs & Interests. Houses numerous clubs dealing with topics ranging from books to ethics to pet care, as well as the American Association for Retired Persons, the American Cancer Society, a cooking club, a ham radio club and more.

Computing. Features software libraries and reviews, user groups, information about computer companies and hardware, a New Product Showcase, *Computer Life Magazine*, *Cobb Group* online and other computer magazines.

Travel. Allows you to see the world through *Fromme's City Guides*, *Fodor's Worldview*, *Travel Holiday Magazine*, the *National Geographic Traveler* and other publications. There's information about bed and breakfasts, and you can use your computer to book airline reservations.

Marketplace. Includes classified ads, car pricing guides and catalogs from FAO Schwartz, Fossil Watches, Godiva Chocolatier, Tower Records, The Sharper Image, JC Penney and others.

People Connection. Allows you to enter chat rooms where you can discuss an incredible variety of subjects over the computer with other AOL subscribers.

Newsstand. Contains an extremely long list of newspapers, magazines and journals, plus syndicated columnists and computer publications.

Entertainment. Offers games, show business news, WEBentertainment, movie reviews and more.

Education. Designed for students. It contains the *Academic Assistance Center*, *Barron's BookNotes*, the *Career Center*, *Columbia Encyclopedia*, *Compton's Encyclopedia*, the *National Academy of Sciences Online*, *National Geographic Online*, the *Library of Congress Online* and *Merriam-Webster Online*. For the college-bound, there's the *College Board Online*, *Simon & Schuster's College Online* and information about financial aid.

Reference Desk. Provides information on various topics, including business, personal finance, computing, geography, travel, government, law, health, the humanities and sciences.

Internet Connection. The gateway to the Internet. You can search the Web with the WebCrawler, download software, join mailing lists, send e-mail throughout the Internet and tap into bulletin boards. (I'll explain what all this means in Chapter 7.)

Sports. Provides news and scores, trivia, statistics, the ABC Sports center and sports chat.

Kids Only. Includes chat rooms, Homework Helpers and other features designed for younger children.

In Chapter 6, we'll take a closer look at how the educational and reference materials in the Newsstand, Education and Reference Desk sections can help high school and college students.

Prodigy

Prodigy, which has over two million subscribers, is a family-oriented online service. Prodigy's features include:

News/weather. The latest news and weather from around the world, plus the ability to search through the Associated Press, Dow Jones and other news services for information.

Business/finance. Regular stock quotes, the status of various economic indicators, news of many companies and other information. There's also an Investment Center, Online Trading and Online Banking.

Sports. The latest scores and statistics, along with ESPN Inside Info, news, contests and polls.

Communications. E-mail, chatting with other members, information about 2,000 topics on over 70 bulletin boards, classified or personal ads and product reviews.

Entertainment. News, games, polls, television gossip and reviews, movies, theater, music and books.

Marketplace. Browse through catalogs from JC Penney, Spiegel and many other stores, then make your purchases over the computer.

Computers. Daily updates from many computer publications, including *PC Week* and *MacWEEK*, software that can be downloaded, opportunities to ask questions, share information and talk with key figures in the computer industry. There's also a Computing Marketplace.

Travel. Columns and tips on business and family travel, and the ability to purchase airline tickets, book hotel rooms and reserve rental cars through the computer.

Kids Zone. Games, stories, humor, contests and activities for kids.

Teen Turf. Games, stories, activities and humor for older children, along with an "Ask Beth" column that answers members' questions.

To aid in research, Prodigy's various sections give you access to: *Compton's Online Encyclopedia, Newsweek, Newsday Direct, Consumer Reports, Kiplinger's, PC World, Mac Home Journal, Advertising Age, PEN, Playbill Online, Sports Illustrated for Kids, The Atlanta Journal Constitution, The Dallas Morning News, The Houston Chronicle* and educational and reference materials. Prodigy also offers Homework Helper, a tool for rapidly gathering information on a topic. You simply type in the subject you're looking for, such as "atoms," and Homework Helper gives you a list of articles about atoms. You can read any of the articles by clicking on them.

eWorld

eWorld is Apple Computer's new online service aimed at families. The opening screen (the first thing you see) is a cartoon-like drawing of a series of cities and towns. The largest of these, a metropolis called Web City, is down the road from the Learning Community.

eWorld's Learning Community, designed for students, parents and teachers, is a miniature city containing News Stand, Museum, School House, Library and Government Center sections.

News Stand. Offers more than 20 newspapers, magazines and other news sources, including the *San Francisco Chronicle*, *Kyodo Cyber Express* (Japan's largest international news agency), *China News Digest* and the *St. Petersburg Press*.

Museum. A super-museum housing art, history, science and cultural museums. The art museum contains electronic images taken from the Louvre, the Dallas Museum of Art, the Arthur Ross Gallery and other fine arts collections. By clicking into the Louvre, you can download color images from "les tres riches heures du Duc de Berry" or many other great works right into your computer, incorporate them into your art report and print them out.

School House. An online resource of elementary, middle and high schools, as well as colleges and universities. Most are in the United States, except the Wangaratta Primary School in Australia, Prague's Charles University and some others. Through the School House you can read campus newspapers, view student art, review courses, look into school libraries and otherwise see what your fellow students are learning and doing.

Library. You'll find *Webster's Dictionary*, various language dictionaries, a thesaurus, *Bartlett's Familiary Quotations*, a guide to colleges, information on World War II, the U.S. Constitution, the Emancipation Proclamation, the Gettysburg Address, book reviews, maps, links to the Library of Congress and many other resources.

Government Center. Allows you to contact and learn about the White House, the Library of Congress, The U.S. House of Representatives, the FBI, Greenpeace, the Libertarian Party and more.

GEnie

General Electric's online service, GEnie, is targeted to businesspeople and researchers. It is divided into special areas called Computing, Family, News & Sports, Career Services, Business, Medicine & Science, Travel, Shopping, Games, Chat, Entertainment and Education. Through GEnie, you can look at *Grolier's Encyclopedia, Medline* (for medical information), *Dun & Bradstreet* and other business and general information resources. Members can also use this service to buy and sell stocks through Charles Schwab.

AT&T Business Network

The AT&T Business Network is a collection of more than 2,500 news and information sources related to business. Through the service, you can obtain information from *CNN Business News, Dow Jones Business Information Services, Dun & Bradstreet Information Services, Entrepreneur Magazine, Kiplinger, Standard & Poors, TRW Business Information Services* and the *Thomas Register of American Manufacturers*.

America Online, Prodigy, eWorld, GEnie and AT&T Business Network are just some of the online services available today. Competition is forcing the online services to constantly add new features and to increase access to the Internet.

There are tolls on the superhighway

The cost of going online? Online time is not free. For example, as of January, 1996:

- America Online charges $9.95 per month, which gets you five "free" hours worth of online time. Additional hours cost $2.95 each.
- CompuServe charges $9.95 per month for five "free" hours and then $2.95/hour. You can opt for the Super-Value Plan: 20 "free" hours per month for $24.95, then $1.95/hour.
- Prodigy's basic plan is $9.95 per month, for five "free" hours, then $2.95/hour. The Value Plan buys you unlimited time on certain features for $14.95 per month, plus five hours worth of time on specific other features. You can also select the 30/30 plan: $29.95 per month buys you 30 hours. With both the Value Plan and 30/30, additional hours cost $2.95.
- Microsoft Network's standard plan costs $4.95 a month for three "free" hours, plus $2.50/hour thereafter. Frequent users can buy 20 hours a month for $19.95.

Bulletin board systems

Requiring little more than a single computer, a modem and a phone line, bulletin board systems (BBSes) have sprung up all over the information superhighway. Some are large and well-designed, while others are tiny, haphazard affairs. Some of the BBSes are on the main byways, others are way out in the boondocks.

BBSes are smaller than the online services, focusing on one or just a few topics. There are BBSes on almost any topic, including:

- *BCS-BBS Line 1,* a bulletin board dedicated to genealogy and the Internet at 407-687-9355.
- *Biz Link BBS,* specializing in business topics at 818-360-9611.
- *Bytewise,* for amateur astronomers and ham radio operators at 908-363-2760.
- *Hillside BBS,* which focuses on topics of interest to Christians at 714-362-9675.
- *Home School,* for those interested in home schooling and education at 407-328-4294.
- *Hookline,* a bulletin board for fans of fishing at 815-727-1195.
- *Kid's World,* a BBS for children at 215-289-6041.
- *Ninth Circle,* a BBS devoted to creative writing and free thought at 205-383-4329.
- *Writer's BBS,* for authors and fans of poetry and literature at 508-481-5478.

In addition to information and discussions, some of the BBSes offer e-mail, software that can be downloaded, access to the Internet and other services.

Online services offer many BBSes. For example, on Prodigy you'll find bulletin boards entitled Adoption, Arts, Astrology & New Age, Automotive, Black Experience, Books & Writing, Canada, Careers, Computer, Cultures, Football, Genealogy, Health, Legal Exchange, Music, Myth & Fantasy, Native American, Parenting, Religion Concourse, Science & Environment, Seniors and Veterans.

Online safety guidelines

The overwhelming majority of people you meet online are friendly and polite. Unfortunately, a very small number of people have used e-mail and "chat" services to take advantage of others. To guard against any trouble, follow these rules:

- Remember that you can't see who you are "talking" to. You don't know if they're really who they say they are, or if they're hiding something from you.
- Do not give out your phone number or address, or any other personal information—including your picture.
- You do not have to respond to messages or questions that make you uncomfortable.
- If someone offends you or sends you objectionable material, just "hang up." If you're using an online service or a BBS, report the problem immediately.
- Children should not arrange to meet face to face with anyone that they've gotten to know online, unless they've discussed the get together with their parents, and a parent goes along. Adults should also exercise caution when meeting online friends for the first time. Treat the encounter cautiously, like a blind date you've arranged through the personal ads.

Chapter 6

Getting answers with America Online

Need help finding information? Have a question that has to be answered right now? Want to take some practice tests to see how much you know? America Online (AOL), one of the major national online services, offers a smorgasbord of information in its Education section. Resources range from the Academic Assistance Center to the *Library of Congress Online* to the *Writer's Club*. There's also *Barron's BookNotes*, the *Columbia Encyclopedia*, the *National Academy of Sciences Online*, *Classical Music Online*, the *Nature Conservancy*, the *National Space Society*, *Compton's Encyclopedia & Forum*, information on college and financial aid, an online campus and a teacher's network.

America Online, Prodigy, CompuServe, eWorld and others have a wealth of information. Since there isn't enough room to describe all of them, I've arbitrarily limited this discussion to America Online. If you decide to sign up with an online service, check them all out to see which has the resources that best suit your needs.

Let's take a look at some of the many ways students can test their knowledge, find answers and hone their learning skills through AOL. Go to the main screen and click on "Education." Then, to get the quickest and most direct answers to your questions, click on the Academic Assistance Center.

Academic assistance

The Academic Assistance Center helps students sharpen their skills and complete their homework. The Center is divided into several areas, including: Teacher Pager, Academic Message Board, Academic Assistance Classrooms, Study Skills Center, Exam Prep Center.

You'll also find Mini-Lesson Libraries, academic contests, *Simon & Schuster's College Online*, *College Board Online*, *Kaplan Online* and other resources. Let's take a closer look at some of the key resources, beginning with the Teacher Pager, the Academic Message Board and the Academic Assistance Classrooms, the three choices on the right side of the Academic Assistance Center screen.

Teacher Pager

Have you ever wished that you had a teacher on call, 24 hours a day, who was just dying to answer your questions? The Teacher Pager is probably the closest most of us will get to that fantasy. You can ask any question you like, on topics ranging from anatomy to zoology.

After clicking on the Teacher Pager button, you select the general area in which your question lies: math, science

or technology, English or foreign language, history and social science or other. Then type in your question, and indi-
cate whether you want the answer to be geared for an
elementary school, middle school, high school or college
student. Your answer will be e-mailed to you within 30
minutes to 24 hours, although 48 hours may be required to
answer more complex questions.

To see how well the Teacher Pager worked, I asked
two questions. Here are my questions and the answers I
received.

I asked this history and social sciences question, requesting a college-level response:

Q: *What was the significance of the Kellogg-Briand Pact of
1938?*

A: The significance was zero. U.S. Secretary of State Kel-
logg and France's Briand wrote a pact that said "all agreed
nations would settle conflicts by peaceful means." It was
signed by 15 nations at first, and later by a total of 62. Unfortunately, the pact had no measure of enforcement. It
was a "feel good" piece of paper. Idealistic but unrealistic.

I asked for a high-school level response to this Math
question:

Q: *What is a quadratic equation?*

A: The online dictionary gives the following definitions:
quadratic: involving terms of the second degree at most.
quadratic form: a homogenous polynomial of the second
degree.
polynomial: a mathematical expression of one or more algebraic terms each of which consists of a constant multi-
plied by one or more variables raised to a non-negative in-
tegral power.

So a quadratic equation is a second degree polynomial. By second degree, I mean that the largest power or exponent is 2.

A quadratic is any equation of the form of:

$$Y \text{ or } f(x) = ax^2 + bx + c$$

where "a," "b" and "c" can be any real number, either positive or negative. Here are some examples of quadratic equations:

$$Y = 3x^2$$
$$Y = x^2 + 4x$$
$$Y = 12x^2 - 7$$

The Teacher Pager is not a substitute for your own study and research, but personalized answers to pressing questions can be a great help.

You may find that your question has already been asked and the answer saved. You can check these out by clicking on "Spotlight on Teacher Pager," which you'll find in the scrollable menu to the left of the "Teacher Spotlight" button.

Here's one of the question/answers:

Q: *Tell me about the poem "The Rhyme of the Ancient Mariner."*

A: This is a narrative poem (one that tells a story) in which an elderly sailor shows up at a wedding party and there recounts to the wedding guests a tale of mishap and recovering. The whole poem is actually a story-within-a-story: There's the story of the Mariner at the wedding, and within that the story of his travels with the albatross and various trials and tribulations. The wedding scene serves as a frame for the main tale.

In this tale the Mariner speaks of how, sometime before, his ship was thrown off course in a storm and driven into the polar regions, where the sailors befriended an albatross (a large seabird) which followed their ship on its journey. The bird was harmless and affectionate, but the Mariner (inexplicably) shoots and kills it. The result appears to be a plague on the ship and its crew: They drift into a hot, windless part of the world, and some of the crew dies of thirst/heatstroke. Most of them believe that the Mariner is to blame; his killing the albatross apparently cursed the ship, so they hang the dead bird around his neck. In the course of their suffering, they are visited by a ship of death, and the Mariner tries to pray.

The Mariner's attempts to repent are useless, until he has an epiphany—a sudden realization and awakening. This comes when he is watching sea creatures in the moonlight, and abruptly "a spring of love" gushes from his heart. In other words, his former act of violence and hostility (killing the albatross) is redeemed when he is infused with sudden love for all things. The albatross falls from his neck, and after a few more trials, he and the surviving crew member make it to their homeland. He is thus compelled to travel the world, recounting his tale. His purpose: to help inspire in others a spirit of communion with and reverence for all living things. That is the only thing that redeems humanity's otherwise sinful or wrongheaded and violent nature.

Many literary critics have seen parallels between this story and the story of Christ: man, in his greed and violence, is cursed by God and cast from the garden; his only redemption is through Christ, emblematic of love for humanity. Error—resulting in suffering—and redemption through humility and love is a typical pattern found in both religious stories and literature.

This brief essay doesn't answer all possible questions about the Ancient Mariner's story, but it gives a brief summary and raises some interesting questions—enough to get you started in your research. Other saved question/answer sets include:

- How are arches constructed?
- How is wind made?
- Is there intelligent life on planets past Pluto?
- The causes of the Civil War.
- The effect of salt on plants.
- What are tilapia?
- Where did the name Earth come from?
- Why aren't the continents called islands?

Academic Message Board

For less pressing problems, and for an opportunity to hear from other students as well as from teachers, you can post a question on the Academic Message Board. The message boards are similar to chat rooms, but tend to be more focused and academically oriented—it's like asking your study group for help. Some questions receive one or just a few answers, while others provoke an ongoing dialogue. America Online's teachers reply to many of the questions, often pointing out resources to explore. Here are just two of the many questions and answers posted:

Q: *I'm doing a report on the invention of the transistor. If anyone has any information, please send it.*

A: Physicists John Bardeen, William B. Shockley and Walter Brattain shared the 1956 Nobel Prize for jointly inventing the transistor. For complete information, please use keyword WEB and enter this address: *http://www. invent.org/book/book-text/5.html.*

Q: *I'm looking for any information I can find for a career report on anesthesiology.*

A: Go to Keyword: Webcrawler and do a text search with: Anesthesiology. There are 185 documents.

Just as you do when asking classmates for help, you have to carefully consider the replies you receive on the Message Board. Just because an answer has been posted doesn't mean it's right!

Academic Assistance Classrooms

The third way to get answers is to go "back to class" in the Academic Assistance Classrooms—live chat areas with teachers on hand to answer questions. There are five areas, covering:

- Math.
- History, plus the social sciences and law.
- Science and medicine.
- English, literature and foreign languages.
- All other subjects, including help preparing for tests.

"Teachers" are on duty in the Academic Assistance Center from 4 p.m. to 2 a.m. Eastern time, and may be available at other times of the day. Simply go to the right room and ask your question. (Unfortunately, the "right" teacher may not be in the classroom when you are. But it's worth a try.)

After you've tried "live" help...

The Teacher Pager, Academic Message Board and Academic Assistance Classrooms give live, rapid (maybe even instant) feedback. But there are plenty of other ways to get information.

After you've tried the pager, board and classrooms, check into the choices listed in the scrollable menu to the left of the Academic Assistance screen. You'll find Homework Helpers, Mini-Lessons and much more.

Homework Helpers

Homework Helpers are mini-essays on a variety of topics, including chemistry, physics, biology, math, Greek and Roman gods, the American Revolution, Shakespeare and European history.

To get to Homework Helpers, click on "AAC News." A new window, titled AAC News and Information will appear. Homework Helpers are the second item in the new window. Scroll through the subjects listed and choose the one that will help you. You'll find information on:

- Adding negative and positive integers.
- Ancient Greek knowledge.
- Exponents.
- Finding logarithms.
- King Tut.
- Newton's Laws.
- Prime factorization.
- Probability.
- Quadratic equations.
- Surface areas and volumes of shapes.

- The code of Hammurabi.
- The Great Pyramids.
- The Pythagorean Theory.
- The Seven Ancient Wonders.
- The speed of sound in water.
- What is beyond space.

   ...and much more.

Mini-lesson libraries

Here you can download numerous mini-lessons on a variety of subjects including: algebraic equations, American Gothic, arches in architecture, Battle of Gettysburg, beta decay, black holes, city life in the Middle Ages, famous composers, General John Burgoyne, graphing linear equations, gravity, Greek/Roman gods, hemophilia, Iran in the Cold War, kinetic energy, King Henry I, logarithms and statistics, lunar eclipses, Mayan Indians, NeoNazism, personal hygiene in outer space, physics, Romanticism and Impressionism, Salvador Dali's childhood, The Milky Way, theater trends in the 1980s, Thomas Alva Edison, World War I and British classes.

Barron's BookNotes

Although it's best to read the entire book, condensed versions with commentary, such as Barron's BookNotes, can be helpful study aids. The brief summaries and questions they pose can stimulate your thinking.

A typical guide looks at many aspects of a work. For example, the guide to *Macbeth* covers the plot, Macbeth himself, Lady Macbeth (his wife and partner in crime), Banquo (his fellow general and friend upon whom he turns), the witches who set the action in motion by foretelling the future, Malcolm and Duncan (sons of the king he slays), the setting and themes, form and structure, Shakespeare's sources, changes in the meanings of words since *Macbeth* was written and more.

Each BookNote includes a biography of the author whose work is under discussion, literary criticism of the work, plus an analysis of the work's characters, plot and other qualities. AOL has many of the BookNotes, including *The Aeneid, A Farewell to Arms, Anna Karenina, Beowulf,*

Brave New World, Canterbury Tales, Crime and Punishment, The Crucible, Death of a Salesman, Don Quixote, Grapes of Wrath, Great Expectations, Hamlet, The Iliad, Jane Eyre, Lord Jim, Lord of the Flies, Moby Dick, The Red Badge of Courage, The Scarlet Letter, Slaughterhouse-Five, The Sun Also Rises, A Tale of Two Cities and others—more than enough to get you through any English literature class!

The Odyssey Project

If you want to get information on a "visual" topic, the kind you might see in *National Geographic*, investigate The Odyssey Project. The Odyssey Project puts pictures above the words to describe what it's like to hold a baby chimpanzee while floating down the Zaire River, to enter into a shark's cave near the Yucatan Peninsula or clamber up and down Andean mountains looking for dinosaur footprints.

You can take a computer odyssey to study Kenya, the great white shark, the Mississippi River, Bali, Christmas in New York or take a special trip back to 1627.

Putting it all together

How do you draw these resources together to find what you need, quickly? Let's say you were doing a report on the heart. You could work your way through the Reference Newsstand and Education sections, looking at the encyclopedias, health magazines and other references. Or, you could type in the keyword "Health" and be taken right to the Health screen, where you find AOL's health resources gathered together.

Now you can investigate the Community Forum, the Better Health & Medical Forum, References, Magazines and News or move into the Internet.

If you open the Heart & Circulatory selection under the scrollable Community Forum list, you'll find a wealth of information on heart and circulatory system disorders, including:

- ACE inhibitors.
- Aneurysms.
- Beta blocker drugs.
- Cardiovascular parts.
- Coronary artery disease.
- Diuretics.
- Glaucoma.
- Headaches, migraine and cluster.
- Heart attack.
- Heart healthy food choices.
- Heart valves.
- High blood cholesterol.
- High blood pressure.
- Kawasaki syndrome.
- Mitral valve prolapse.
- Stroke.
- Thrombophlebitis.
- Varicose veins.
- Vein clots.
- Ventricular premature beats.

You can also read the messages and replies posted, or post one of your own.

The Better Health and Medicine Forum allows you to search the online Health Forum and participate in chats on mental health, addiction, sexuality, health reform and other topics. The Forum also has a section on Alternative Medicine Information where you can research a large number of heart-related topics, including acupressure, acupuncture, aromatherapy, the Alexander Technique, biological rhythms, chiropractic, holistic medicine, homeopathy, naturopathy and vegetarian diets.

The Forum also includes a library of health and heart-related software you can download into your computer, a chat room devoted to heart disease, message boards and other information.

Use Your Computer

The Heart Message Board is an excellent way to gather information by asking questions and exchanging information in discussion and support groups covering a wide variety of topics, from angina to strokes and surgery.

Speaking to others who share your interest can help you cut through a lot of preliminary research and get right to the "heart" of the matter.

- If you select Magazines, you can read *Scientific American*, *Longevity* and other health magazines.

- In the Reference area you can browse through encyclopedias, search a comprehensive medical database called *Medline*, look up more than 9,000 drugs in *Consumer Reports Complete Drug Reference* and get definitions from *Merriam-Webster's Medical Dictionary*.

- News presents the latest health information from around the world, taken right from Reuters news service.

- Top Internet Sites takes you into the Internet, where you can cruise on over to health-related Web pages.

- Online Events include a potpourri of health-related chats and discussions. The topics change from time to time, so there may not be one on the heart when you're doing your research. However, if you begin your project early, you can start your own forum by requesting one. If enough people join, you'll have your own discussion group to provide you with information about your topic.

If you still don't have enough information for your report, you can always ask for more guidance by speaking to a teacher via Teacher Pager.

With all these resources—ranging from a definition of the heart in *Merriam-Webster's Medical Dictionary* to the scientific journals in *Medline* to speaking with heart patients—most students will find what they need.

Studying how to study online

Learning how to study more effectively, finding answers and getting help with problem areas can smooth the way for any student. Those who need a little extra, well-focused help can find that, too, by looking in the Study Skills Service. For example, if you're in an English class, you'll find lots of appropriate help with:

- Choosing between "who" and "whom."
- Boundaries between sentences.
- Linking independent clauses.
- Parallel content and phrasing.
- Comma placement.

- Maximizing your learning.
- Separating and linking sentences.
- Writing the exploratory essay.
- Writing to bridge cultures.

Testing your knowledge

AOL presents "How Much Do You Know?" quizzes in the form of contests, with winners receiving free computer time. They're good for two reasons: you get to test your knowledge, and you learn as you play. You'll find the quizzes in the Brain Bowl. Can you answer these questions?

- Do mosquitoes have teeth?
- What is the smallest bone in the human body?
- Who was the first black person to be named to a job by a United States president?

- Why did George Bernard Shaw turn down England's prestigious Order of Merit?
- Who coined the term "willing suspension of disbelief" and to what does it refer?
- How do monolayer and multilayer trees differ in form? Where would you find each type?
- I have just identified Scytonema after returning from a field trip. What is it, where am I and what am I doing?

Learning about universities

If you're close to graduating from high school or college, you may also want to learn as much as you can about colleges or graduate schools to which you may be applying.

Here is an example of what you can learn about a particular university, such as the University of Texas, Austin, also known as UT:

- It is a 4-year coed public university, founded in 1883, located in Austin, the capital of Texas. Regionally accredited. On the semester system, with a full summer school schedule. The campus boasts a fusion reactor, scientific and humanities research centers, an observatory, art galleries and the Lyndon Baines Johnson Library and Museum.
- There are 10,000 computers on campus and in the dormitories.
- There are 15,770 male and 14,247 female full-time undergraduates, and 2,739 male and 2,450 female part-time undergraduates.
- Of those who apply, 65 percent are accepted, with acceptance based on grades, test scores, recommendations, activities, essay and talents.

- The university offers BA, BS, BFA, BArch, MA, MS, MBA, MFA, MEd, PhD, EdD, Pharm D and JD degrees.
- There are close to 100 undergraduate majors, including accounting, aerospace, American studies, astronomy, biology, chemistry, computer and information sciences, dance, economics French, geology, interior design, journalism and mass communications, marine/aquatic biology, mathematics, molecular biology, music history and literature, petroleum engineering, philosophy, physics, radio and television broadcasting, sociology, Spanish and zoology.
- Dormitories, apartments, fraternities and sororities are available for student living.
- Student activities include the student newspaper and yearbook, intercollegiate and intramural sports, drama, choral groups, pep band, orchestra and over 40 clubs, plus political, ethnic, religious, social service and other organizations.

Entrance requirements, application process, fees and financial aid are also discussed.

And that's just the beginning

AOL has an exam preparation center, and fee-charging online courses in a variety of subjects. (For a fee, you can hook up with Kaplan and other test-preparation services).

These are just some of the resources available on America Online. Now let's look at the educational resources available on the Internet itself.

Chapter 7

Surf's up on the Internet

The Internet—that vast, mysterious collection of computer networks linking every corner of the globe—is a cornucopia of facts, statistics, documents, opinions, arguments, lists, video and sound clips. The answer to most any question is on the Internet—somewhere. The only trick is to find it.

As you recall from Chapter 5, the Internet is a gigantic network made up of computer networks, sub-networks and sub-sub-networks, down to individual computers that have been set up as information-dispensing hosts. Although the Internet can be intimidating, it's actually quite easy to use, thanks to the Web and other programs that serve as super card catalogues.

Learning the Internet lingo

You'll come across many abbreviations as you search for information. Fortunately, you don't have to know what many of them mean. (They're usually just abbreviations or

names of individual computers, companies or individuals).
But there are some you should know, including:

- **com.** An abbreviation indicating that the addressee is a commercial service.
- **edu.** An abbreviation indicating that the addressee is an educational institution.
- **FAQ.** Frequently Asked Questions (and their answers) that are often available for you to peruse.
- **ftp.** File transfer protocol is like a standardized "language" which can be used by all of the many different types of computers on the Internet.
- **gopher.** Developed at the University of Minnesota, home of the fighting Golden Gophers, a gopher is a special program that "burrows" through mountains of information, arranging a bewildering array of Internet addresses into a simple menu. With a gopher you can select your choices from the menu, rather than having to burrow through the maze of computers yourself.
- **gov.** An abbreviation indicating that the addressee is a governmental agency.
- **homepage.** The "directory" or "receptionist" of an information site on the World Wide Web.
- **HTML.** HyperText Markup Language, a standard language used for documents on the Web.
- **http.** HyperText Transport Protocol, which allows you to jump from one linked document to the next.
- **link.** An invisible connection between one document and another. Typically, a home page will have a series of words and/or images that are linked to other documents. Selecting any of these causes the information you want to be retrieved automatically.
- **mailing list.** Asking to be put on a mailing list is like signing up for a "subscription" to everything posted to a particular discussion group. Request the mailing list manager to add your name to the list, and soon you'll receive e-mail copies of everything posted to the group.

- **mil.** An abbreviation indicating that the addressee is part of the military.
- **net.** An abbreviation indicating that the addressee is an Internet provider.
- **newsgroup.** A Usenet (see definition below) term used to describe an electronic "bulletin board" filled with questions, answers, statements, lists and other contributions. The contributions, all devoted to the newsgroup's topic, are posted by members of the group for all to read. Alternative newsgroups, which include "alt" in their address, may look at racier subjects.

   To help clear the clutter, the thousands of newsgroups are divided into hierarchies according to general topic. "Comp" in the newsgroup's name means that it's devoted to computers, "rec" means recreation and sports, "sci" means science and scholarly topics, "soc" means social issues, "talk" means discussions of current issues and "misc" covers everything else.
- **org.** An abbreviation indicating that the addressee is an organization.
- **URL.** Universal (or Uniform) Resource Locator— "addresses" that manage searching, moving and retrieving information on the Web.
- **Usenet.** A group of computer networks that host and share information from an unknown but large number of newsgroups.
- **Web, World Wide Web (WWW).** A tool that allows you to search for information on the Internet.

The student's Internet directory

This listing on pages 95 to 104 of Internet sites will get you started in your research. It's not a comprehensive listing of information sites on the Internet, just a little taste of all the delightful information you can gobble up. But remember:

- Some of the sites are informative and well-organized, some are quirky and skimpy.
- Some are well-researched and trustworthy, and some are the rantings of a mad person. Just because you see it on your computer screen doesn't mean that it's the truth.
- Some provide unbiased information with no ulterior motive, some slant their information to sell you on their cause. And some are just offering enough information to entice you to buy something.
- Some are easy to use, some require you to search through listings to find what you need.
- Some have the information, some link you to other sites and some are simply listings of sites.
- And some may be gone when you look for them again. That happens.
- Some are free, but some cost, and cost a lot. Be sure to check out cost before going online.

With all of that in mind, take a look at just a few of the countless sites that can aid the student conducting research on the following selection of topics:

Abortion
- If you're interested in the pro-choice side of the debate, see the *California Abortion and Reproductive Rights Action League Web Page* at http://www.caral.org
- If you want to focus on the prolife side, see the *Baptists for Life* at http://web.wingsbbs.com/b4life/
- For an analysis of both sides, investigate the *Ontario Center for Religious Tolerance*: http://www.kosone.com/people/ocrt/abortion.htm

Use Your Computer

Art

- *Art On the Net* is a virtual gallery for over 50 visual artists, musicians and poets: http://www.art.net/
- Artwork and other resources at the *Smithsonian Institute* can be viewed at http://www.si.edu
- The *Leonardo Da Vinci Museum* presents selected works and a biography: http://www.leonardo.net/museum/main.html
- Many art treasures are on display at *The Louvre:* http://www.paris.org./Musees/Louvre

Astronomy

- Begin your star tours at *AstroWeb,* which links you to many astronomy information sites: http://marvel.stsci.edu/net-resources.html
- You can look through NASA documents at *NASA Information Services:* http://www.nasa.gov/

Biology

- England's *University of Cambridge School of Biological Sciences* contains databases, journals and links to other biology information sites: http://www.bio.cam.ac.uk
- You can look into resources at *WWW Sites for Biologists* at http://www.abc.hu/biosites.html

Business/economics

- The World Bank is filled with information on current business/economics events, information on various countries, publications and current research: http://www.worldbank.org
- Learn about investing by reading *Investment FAQ* at http://www.cis.ohio-state.edu/hypertext/faq/usenet/investment-faq/general/top.html

- Check out *Washington Trade Center* for statistics, information on the Russian economy and more: http://www.eskimo.com/~bwest
- Students of futures can read the rules of trading and get the latest information courtesy of the Chicago Mercantile Exchange at http://nt.scbbs.com/cme

Chemistry

- *Internet Chemistry Resources* has databases, journals, software and much more: http://www.rpi.edu/dept/chem/cheminfo/chemres.html

College/financial aid

- *CollegeNet.* Type in some information on the type of college you're looking for, and you'll receive descriptions of those that fit the bill: http://www.collegenet.com/
- The *Internet College Exchange* has information on selecting and applying to college. It allows you to search for a college or university by name, type, size, location and field of study: http://www.usmall.com/college/
- *ASKERIC.* "ERIC," also known as the Federal Educational Resources Information Center, can point you to many sources of financial aid: http://ericir.syr.edu/
- *The Financial Aid Information Page* will link to you the financial aid departments at many institutes of higher learning: http://www.cs.cmu.edu/afs/cs.cmu.edu/user/mkant/Public/FinAid/finaid.html

Computers

- The *Virtual Computer Library* links you to many hundreds of other computer resources, including magazines, manuals and glossaries: http://www.utexas.edu/computer/vcl/
- You'll find a detailed dictionary at *The Free Online Dictionary of Computing*: http://wombat.doc.ic.ac.uk/

- To learn more about the Internet, try *Zen and the Art of the Internet* at http://www.cs.indiana.edu/docproject/zen/zen-1.0_toc.html

- The *Clearinghouse for Subjects-Oriented Internet Resource Guides* contains guides to locating information on the Internet: http://www.lib.umich.edu/chhome.html

- *Usenet Information Center Launch Pad* gives information on and links to Usenet groups: http://sunsite.unc.edu/usenet-i/home.html

Crime

- Look at the *Justice Information Center,* which has statistics and other information on crime, drugs, the court system, law enforcement and more: http://www.ncjrs.org/

- For links to numerous criminology sites, including international aspects of the discipline, and to download publications on various aspects of law and crime, try the *Institute for Law and Justice* at http:www.iTj.org/

Dance

- Find pictures, dance reviews and links to other dance sites at *Ballet Web:* http://users.aol.com/balletweb/balletweb.html.

- Learn about the *Paris Opera Ballet* at http://www.ens~lyon.fr/~esouche/danse/POB.html

Demography

- Look into the links to demographic information sites at *Demography and Population Studies:* http://coombs.anu.edu.au/ResFacilities/DemographyPage.html

Domestic violence

- For statistics, essays and information about services available for familes, read the *Family Violence Awareness Page* at http://www.iquest.net/~gtemp/famvi.htm

Feminism

- If you want to read or share feminist viewpoints, get on the *FemSuprem* mailing list by sending your e-mail request to: femsuprem-request@resaissoft.com
- To study key feminist issues, tap into the *National Organization of Women* at http://now.org/

Film

- Try the *Internet Movie Database*. You'll find information on over 50,000 movies, along with cast lists, biographies and other information at http://www.msstate.edu/Movies/
- For a list of films in the Library of Congress's National Film Registry, see: gopher://marvel.loc.gov/00/research/reading.rooms/motion.picture/nfpb/nfrnet
- Over 300 movie and 100 television scripts can be downloaded from *Drew's Scripts O-Rama* at http://home.cdsnet.net/~nikko11/scripts.htm. You'll also find screenplays written by little-known authors.

Genetics

- Investigate genetics at the *Exploratorium Explore Net:* http://www.exploratorium.edu/

Geography

- The *WWW Virtual Geography Library* links you to numerous geography resources: http://hpb1.hwc.ca:10002/WWW_VL_Geography.html

Government

- *The Yankee Citizen* looks at the Democratic and Republican parties, and offers information on government: http://www.tiac.net/users/macgyver/pols.html
- The *Heinz Server*, run by Carnegie-Melon's Heinz School of Public Policy and Management, contains resources regarding varous aspects of public policy: http://info.heinz.cmu.edu/
- The *Library of Congress* gives you an opportunity to tap into its card catalogue: http://www.loc.gov
- The *House of Representatives* presents general information, legislation, member profiles and more: http://www.house.gov
- To learn about the upper house of Congress, its history, roster and activities, review the *Senate FTP Site* at ftp://ftp.senate.gov/

Health

- For official health statistics and information on obtaining health publications, try the *CDC Home Page* at http://www.cdc.gov/cdc.html (CDC stands for the Centers For Disease Control).
- For information and links to other Internet sources of information on health and fitness, try the *Internet Health Resources* at http://www.ihr.com/
- Contact the *National Health Information Center* to find the government office or private health organization that can answer your health questions: http://nhic-nt.health.org/
- The National Institutes of Health are represented on the *NIH Home Page:* http://www.nih.gov
- The *United States Public Health Service* offers news and press releases from the Food & Drug Administration and other government health agencies: http://phs.os.dhhs.gov/phs/phs.html

- The Arthritis Foundation offers information via its *Arthritis Today*: http://www.enews.com/magazines/at/
- Study diabetes courtesy of the *American Diabetes Association* http://www.diabetes.org/

History

- To learn about ancient Greeks, Romans and others, look into *The Ancient World Web* at http://atlantic.evsc.virginia.edu/julia/AncientWorld.html
- *A Timeline of the Counter Culture* looks at the history of contrary ideas from Medieval times to the present at: gopher://gopher.well.sf.ca.us/11/Community/60sTimeline
- *History* covers everything from Rome to the modern era in an extensive collection of articles: http://english-server.hss.cmu.edu/History.html

Human rights

- For links to *Human Rights Watch, Physicians for Human Rights* and other human rights organizations, try gopher://gopher.humanrights.org:5000/
- The *Directory of Human Rights Sites On the Internet* leads you to information on political prisoners, refugees and other persecuted persons around the world: http://www.aaas.org/spp/dspp/shr/dhr.htm
- For documents on the political and legal aspects of human rights, see the *Human Rights Web* at http://www.traveller.com/~hrweb/hrweb.html

International affairs

- For information on countries, government, international organizations and much more, look into the *International Affairs Resources* of the World Wide Web Virtual Library at: http://www.pitt.edu/~ian/ianres.html

- If the North Atlantic Treaty Organization is the object of your research, try the *Nato Gopher* at: gopher:// gopher.nato.int/
- You'll find documents discussing the history and goals of the UN, plus information about what the organization is doing at *United Nations:* http:// www.un.org/

Literature

- Begin with *The Internet Public Library* to find links to author sites online: http://ipl.sils.umich.edu/
- You'll find *The Complete Works of William Shakespeare* at http://the-tech.mit.edu/Shakespeare/works.html
- You'll find novels, poems, articles, letters and other works of literature from the great authors and thinkers of English, French, German, Classical Latin and other worlds at *Carrie,* a full-text electronic library, at: http:// www.ukans.edu/carrie/carrie_main.html
- The works of *Walt Whitman* can be read at: http:// www.cc.columbia.edu/acis/bartleby/whitman/index.html
- The *Isaac Asimov Home Page* contains a comprehensive collection of catalogues, reviews, links and more, from chemistry to science fiction: http://www.clark.net/pub/ edseiler/WWW/asimov_home_page.html

Mathematics

- The *American Mathematical Society* allows you to read documents and link to other sites at http:// e-math.ams.org
- Study the *Most Common Mistakes In College Mathematics* at http://math.vanderbilt.edu/~schectex/ commerrs/
- The *Mathematics Information Server* connects you to virtual libraries, gophers, bulletin boards and other mathematics resources from around the world: http:// www.math.psu.edu/OtherMath.html

Physics

- The *CTI Centre For Physics* home page is a useful starting point when searching for material related to university level physics education: http://www.ph.surrey.ac.uk/cti/home.html

- The *AIP Physics Information NETsite* links you to databases, the *AIP Center for the History of Physics Newsletter* and more: http://www.aip.org/aiphome.html

Politics

- Republicans may want to start their research at the *Republican Central Committee* site: http://republicans.org/

- The *Democratic National Committee* offers press releases, audio clips and more at http://www.democrats.org

- *The Greens Index* describes the development and ideals of Green politics, including the latest developments and future agenda at http://www.dru.nl/maatschappij/politiek/groenen/intlhome.htm

- To learn about the Libertarian Party, look into *Freedom Links* at http://pages.nyu.edu/~dap0686/freedom.html

Reference

- For a fee, you can use *Britannica On-line* at http://www.eb.com/

- Science students may find answers in the *History of Science, Technology and Medicine* at http://www.asap.unimelb.edu.au/hstm/hstm_ove.htm _

- If you want to know what others have said about something, look it up in *Bartlett's Familiar Quotations* at: http://www.cc.columbia.edu/acis/bartleby/bartlett

- If you want to find an alternate way of saying something, try *Roget's Thesaurus* at: gopher://odie.niaid.nih.gov/77/.thesaurus/index

- A wide variety of books can be found courtesy of the *Internet Public Library* at http://ipl.sils.umich.edu/
- You can read the classics in English or their original language courtesy of *The Tech Classics Archive* at http://the-tech.mit.edu/Classics

Religion

- The *Ontario Centre for Religious Tolerance* covers religious freedom, religious abuse and many other issues: http://www.kosone.com/people/ocrt/

Space

- Learn about space travel, from how astronauts are selected to how to eat in space, through *Liftoff to Space Exploration* at http://astro-2.msfc.nasa.gov/

Theatre

- Learn about operetta masters Gilbert and Sullivan and their work at the *Gilbert and Sullivan Archive:* http://diamond.idbsu.edu/GaS/GaS.html
- If you're studying Broadway musical lyrics and can't quite remember them, look into the Tower Lyrics Archive at http://www.ccs.neu.edu/home/tower/lyrics.html

These are just some of the thousands of information sites on the Internet. The amount of information that eager, adventurous students can find is practically unlimited.

Chapter 8

Understanding computer-ese

The computer world is filled with abbreviations, jargon and technical terms, most of which can be safely ignored by most of us. Here's a look at 136 computer terms you should know. (Words in italics have their own, full definitions elsewhere in this chapter.)

access to use your computer to "get into" another computer and use its programs, *download* or read its files, or *upload* material of your own. For example, *online services* such as America Online give you access to the *Internet*.

address the name/location of a computer or user. "letters@news latimescom" is the address of the *Los Angeles Times* "Letters to the Editor" section.

alt this abbreviation identifies a *Usenet newsgroup* that has decided not to participate in the standardized creating and naming system. ("Alt" can also refer to the "alt key" on a keyboard.)

American Standard Code for Information Exchange also known as ASCII (pronounced "ask-key"), is a standardized method of converting characters into the binary code that computers can work with.

applet a small, limited *program* that usually assists or works with other, larger programs.

application see program.

Archie a *program* that helps you find files and directories on other people's computers. Available for free, it was developed at McGill University.

archive a "bank" of files or collections of files. Also, a file or group of files that has been "squashed down" in size for storage. Before you can read or otherwise use the files, you have to use one of many utility programs to "unsquash" the file or files.

ASCII see American Standard Code for Information Exchange.

attached file/attached document a file attached or linked to an *e-mail* message. Typically, the message will say something like "Bob, see the attached file." Then Bob has to open the attached file and read it.

BB see Bulletin Board.

binary code the "language" computers understand, composed of only two characters: "1" and "0."

bit the smallest unit of information in the binary system computers use. A bit is either a "1" or a "0" (an "on" or an "off" in *binary* computer language). Strings of "1s" and "0s" are used to represent all the letters, numbers and other characters used by a computer. Eight bits make a *byte*. "Bit" stands for "*bi*nary dig*it*."

bits per second abbreviated as bps, a measure of speed used to determine how fast information is transferred by a *modem*. Where 2,400 bps was once considered pretty zippy, 14,400 bps is now considered a decent speed. But 28,800 bps modems are becoming common, and will undoubtedly be considered obsolete in no time at all.

Boolean operator word such as "and" or "or" that helps you focus your computer searches. Let's say that you were looking for articles and documents discussing Abraham Lincoln's Gettysburg Address. If you searched for "Abraham Lincoln," you would get a long list of documents relating to Lincoln, many containing nothing about the Gettysburg Address. If you used "and," asking the computer to search for "Abraham Lincoln and Gettysburg Address," only documents that related to both subjects would be identified on your list.

bps see bits per second.

browser a program that helps you find information.

buffer a "holding tank" where data is temporarily stored. If a printer has a buffer, the computer can transfer a lot of information rapidly, then go on to other tasks while the printer turns information in the buffer into printed pages at a more leisurely pace.

bug a software error or problem.

Bulletin Board (BB) a computer that acts as a message center. People can log onto the board to read or leave messages. Some bulletin boards also allow you to send and receive *e-mail, download* software or perform other tasks.

byte made up of eight *bits,* a byte is a standard unit for measuring computer information.

> 8 bits = 1 byte
> 1,024 bytes = 1 kilobyte, or "K"
> 1,024 K = 1 megabyte, or "MG"
> 1,024 MG = 1 gigabyte

cache memory, either in *RAM* or on the hard disc, where information is temporarily stored (pronounced "cash").

case-sensitive the ability to tell the difference between capital and lower case letters. A case-sensitive program insists that you type in the request or address with the proper capital and non-capital letters.

Use Your Computer

CD-ROM a round disc that looks just like CDs that play music, but is actually a computer disc read by a laser in the computer.

client a program on your computer that gets information off another computer, called a *server,* at your request. You tell your client program what you want. The client then asks the *server* on the appropriate computer to provide that information. *Gopher* is a widely-used client program.

clone a piece of computer *hardware* that acts much like the original and more expensive hardware that it mimics.

com a top-level domain name assigned to commercial online services in the *domain name system.*

comp this abbreviation identifies a Usenet newsgroup dedicated to discussing computers.

compatible gets along with, is able to work with. Compatible computers can work with each other. Software that is compatible with a type of computer can be installed and will run on that computer.

CWIS Campus Wide Information System.

cyberspace the "world" created by computers, computer systems and networks, the information they contain and the people who add, exchange and study that information.

database a wealth of information, stored on a *disc* or *hard drive,* that can be easily organized, displayed and printed in many different ways by the proper *software.* The word "database" is also used to describe the programs that handle the storage and organizational tasks.

debug the process of looking for and eliminating the *bugs* that make your software or computer dysfunctional.

desktop publishing using a personal computer and printer to produce professional-looking reports, newsletters, books, etc.— things that used to require a big printing press.

disk drive a piece of *hardware,* either inside or outside of the computer, used to "read" information off of and "write" information on a *disc.*

Disk Operating System also known as DOS, a popular *operating system* used for IBM-compatible computers. It requires some study to operate DOS, and *Windows* can be "superimposed" on DOS to make it more *friendly.*

domain name system a "smaller to bigger" system of allocating names on the Internet. A domain name contains at least three parts: the user, one or more sub-domains and the domain (read from left to right). For example, in this fictional address: john@whuedu—"john" is the name of a particular student, "whu" stands for West Hills University, and "edu" is the top-level domain name assigned to educational institutions in the United States. Domain names can be long and complex.
You can't always tell by looking what all the abbreviations stand for, although the last one, representing the top-domain, is usually one of six if the address is for a location in the United States:

"com" = a commercial service (such as Prodigy)
"edu" = an educational institution
"gov" = the government
"mil" = the military
"net" = an Internet provider
"org" = an organization

There may be all sorts of strange abbreviations, slashes, dots and dashes, but the basic structure remains the same—you're moving from the smaller to the larger entity as you read from left to right.

DOS see Disk Operating System.

download to transfer a file, program or other data from another computer which has been "hooked" to yours by *modem.* The opposite of *upload.*

edu a top-level domain name assigned to educational institutions in the *domain name system.*

e-mail short for electronic mail. Consists of notes, letters and other brief documents sent from one computer user to another.

electronic text also known as e-text, the text of a published or unpublished work that you can access with a computer. Many notable works, including Shakespeare's plays, have been put on computer and are available as electronic text.

file server a computer that has been designated as the "home" for popular files. For example, a file server on a *local area network* may house a giant database that other computers on the network frequently access.

file transfer protocol abbreviated ftp, a system (protocol) for exchanging files on the Internet.

flame a nasty message sent via e-mail. Highly rude, often inflammatory or harassing.

floppy disc a round, bendable magnetic disc, encased in a harder shell, used to store information.

friendly easy-to-use computer software, hardware or operating systems that almost anyone can use.

FTP see file transfer protocol.

gbps gigabytes per second. See gigabyte.

gigabyte a measure of the speed at which data is being transferred, equal to about one billion *bits per second*

gopher a specialized program that simplifies the task of locating resources on the Internet. A gopher automatically contacts other computers and issues the proper commands for you when you have indicated what you'd like to look for.

gov a top-level domain name assigned to the government in the *domain name system*.

Graphic User Interface also known as GUI, a program that allows you to use a *mouse* or other *pointing device* to give instructions to a computer (rather than typing in instructions).

hard drive essentially a large *floppy disc* used for long-term information storage. The hard disc can be *internal* (placed inside the computer) or *external* (sitting in a box of its own next to the computer). Also commonly, but erroneously, called a hard disc. (The disc is the round flat item inside the drive upon which the information is actually encoded.)

hardware the *monitor, hard drive, keyboard* and other parts of the computer that you can touch.

homepage a "directory" or "receptionist" for an information site on the Internet.

HTML see HyperText Markup Language.

hypertext a method of presentation and linking that allows you to jump from place to place within a document, or between documents. Suppose you're reading about World War II on your computer screen: World War II officially began when *Hitler* invaded *Poland* in 1939." Notice that the words "Hitler" and "Poland" are in italics (anchor words). If this explanation of World War II were written in hypertext, you could jump to further discussions of these anchor words by clicking your mouse or pushing a key. Once you've studied the new presentations, you could easily return to your starting place. The anchors can be text, pictures, images or buttons.

hypertext markup language also known as html, a standardized way of describing the way computer documents "look" (their fonts, alignment, indentation, etc.). Used for *hypertext* documents on the *Web*.

icon a little picture on the computer screen that represents an item (such as a file or a hard drive) or a command (such as "print" or "delete").

Information Superhighway the very informal, global connection of computer networks. Government agencies, universities, libraries, museums, companies, private parties and other organizations and individuals have all "hooked up" and made themselves part.

input information that you put into the computer by way of the *keyboard, printer, mouse* or other input device. When you type a report on a computer, the words you type are the input.

Internet a global *network* of computer networks, originally set up and used by the U.S. Department of Defense. Today, it consists of countless networks and sub-networks which use standard *protocols* to talk to each other and allow information to be transferred from one computer to another.

joystick a lever sticking up out of a box or platform that, when pushed one way or the other, causes the *cursor* to move about the screen.

keyboard a rectangular board with rows of letters, numbers and function keys that allow you to type out instructions or enter text into the computer. A keyboard is the primary *input* device that we use to give instructions to a computer.

key word a word that describes or summarizes the topic or contents of a document. When looking for information on the Internet, you may request a key word search for "Hamlet" to find information on Shakespeare's play.

kbps kilobits per second. See kilobyte.

kilobyte about one thousand *bits per second,* a measure of the speed at which data is being transferred.

LAN see local area network.

link a connection between *hypertext* documents, or different parts of the same document, that allows you to quickly and easily jump from place to place or document to document.

local area network also known as LAN, a network made up of computers and *workstations* that are physically close to each other, often within the same department or building.

local newsgroup a *Usenet newsgroup* available only to a certain, limited area (such as a particular university or state).

mail server a term used to describe both a computer that stores and distributes *e-mail,* and a program that handles requests for e-mail.

mainframe a large computer that serves as the "brain" for multiple computer terminals. Typically, there are several "dumb terminals," consisting of a screen and keyboard, attached to the mainframe. People type into individual "dumb terminal" keyboards and see the results on their screens, but the actual computing is done by the mainframe.

mbps megabits per second. See megabyte.

megabyte a measure of the speed at which data is being transferred, equal to about one million *bits per second.*

menu a list of choices.

mil a top-level domain name assigned to the military in the *domain name system.*

mips short for million instructions per second, a unit of measure used to time *central processing units.*

modem a device that converts a computer's signals into a form that can travel through the phone system. The modem modulates (modifies) computer signals before they enter the phone system and after they exit. The word "Modem" stands for "modulator/ demodulator."

moderated newsgroup a *Usenet newsgroup* that has a human being screen all postings to get rid of those that do not relate to the newsgroup's topic, or are otherwise objectionable.

Mosaic a popular browser for the World Wide Web.

multimedia using various text, graphics, sound and video to display information.

multitasking asking the computer to do two or more things at once (such as printing one document while you work on another).

Net see Internet.

net a top-level domain name assigned to Internet access providers in the *domain name system*.

netiquette the suggested rules of behavior to follow while on the *Internet*. They include reading the *Frequently Asked Questions* before posting a question and refraining from issuing a *flame*.

Netscape Navigator a popular *browser* for the *World Wide Web*.

network two or more computers that have been connected and can "talk" to each other, exchange information or share software and/or hardware.

newbie an Internet novice.

news identifies a *Usenet newsgroup* dedicated to discussing Usenet.

newsgroup an ongoing *Usenet* group dedicated to discussing a particular issue over the computer. Members post messages to the newsgroup, which can be read and replied to by all. Each identifies itself as belonging to a particular broad topic. The abbreviations that begin the newsgroup's names are:

> "comp" for computers
> "news" for the Usenet
> "rec" for recreation, hobbies, sports
> "sci" for scientific and scholarly topics
> "soc" for social issues
> "talk" for current and/or controversial issues

A large number of "alternative" newsgroups have opted out of the standardized naming and creation system. They're identified as "alt" groups. Often controversial, they are only available at sites that specifically request them.

offline not connected to the computer or computer network.

online connected to other computers or a computer network. You can be connected to nearby computers by cable, or to distant ones via the telephone wires. Online also describes a "dumb" computer terminal, consisting of a screen and keyboard, that has no computing power of its own, but must be online to draw on a distant *central processing unit*.

operating system *software* that tells the computer *hardware* what to do—how to run programs, control the flow of information, etc. *DOS* is a popular operating system for IBM-compatible computers.

org a top-level domain name assigned to organizations in the *domain name system*.

output the display on the screen, the printed document or other information produced by the computer.

output device a printer, screen, speech synthesizer or any other device that allows the computer to communicate with humans.

PC see personal computer.

peripherals printers, modems and other pieces of *hardware* that are not part of, but are controlled by, the *central processing unit*.

personal computer a computer, generally small enough to fit on a desk, meant to be used by one person at a time. Also known as PC (see *mainframe*).

pixel "dots" of light on the computer screen, turned on and off in specific patterns in order to "show pictures" of what you're typing or drawing on the screen.

printer an *output* device that turns computer information into a printed page of text and/or graphics.

program a set of instructions to the computer that makes it do something. For example, a spreadsheet program instructs the computer to display a series of rows and columns on the screen and to manipulate the data in the rows and columns at your request. Also known as an application.

protocol a rule or procedure which determines how information will be sent from computer to computer. For example, *file transfer protocol* regulates the way files are transferred between computers on the *Internet*.

RAM see random access memory.

Use Your Computer

Random Access Memory also known as RAM, a temporary "storage room" where the *central processing unit* stores information it needs to keep near at hand. The information in RAM keeps changing as the central processing unit adds new, necessary data, and deletes the old. As soon as you turn your computer off, all the information in RAM vanishes.

read only a file that can be opened, read and printed, but not altered or deleted.

rec identifies a *Usenet newsgroup* dedicated to discussing recreation, hobbies and sports.

scan to transfer text or images on paper into the computer by converting them into a digital code that the computer can understand. Comparable to taking a photocopy of the text or image and saving it in the computer.

scanner a *peripheral* device used to convert text or images on a paper into a digital code that the computer can use to reproduce the text or image.

sci identifies a *Usenet newsgroup* dedicated to discussing scientific and scholarly topics.

server a program that handles requests from *client* programs. The server on your computer asks the client what it wants, then fulfills the request.

shareware software that you can try out for free. If you wish to continue using it, you pay the shareware's owner or distributor.

shouting using all capitals letters in *e-mail*, as if you were shouting at someone.

soc identifies a *Usenet newsgroup* dedicated to discussing social issues.

software a computer *program* that tells a computer what you want it to do.

spreadsheet a program that allows you to perform mathematical operations on numbers arranged in rows and columns.

subject tree a tool, such as *Yahoo,* available on the *World Wide Web* that organizes *Internet* resources into categories/subcategories.

surf to roam through the Internet, freely following any *links* or *threads* that catch your attention.

talk identifies a *Usenet newsgroup* dedicated to discussing current and/or controversial issues.

terminal a "dumb" computer that has no computing ability of its own. Simply a keyboard and monitor attached to a computer that does all the work.

thread a series of *Usenet newsgroup* postings that continue a particular discussion. For example, if someone posts a question about Disneyland, all the discussion generated by that posting is part of the Disneyland thread. Threaded newsreaders such as "tm" or "tin" allow you to pluck out and read only those postings related to what you're interested in.

uniform resource locator also known as universal resource locator and URL, a standardized way of telling the computer where you would like to go. It's an address for items on the Web and Internet. There are four parts to a URL. First comes the transfer format, such as "http" for the World Wide Web, or "gopher" when using a gopher. Next is the name of the host computer, such as "www.nytimes" for *The New York Times.* Third is the directory path in the host computer, and finally the name of the file you want to look at.

UNIX a *operating system* developed by AT&T in the late 1960s.

upload to transfer files from your computer to another.

URL see uniform resource locator.

Usenet a large *network* of computers, mostly operating on *UNIX,* that support a large body of *newsgroups.* Many Usenet computers are on the Internet, but Usenet itself is not part of the Internet. Usenet newsgroups are divided into world newsgroups and alternative newsgroups. The world newsgroups follow Usenet standards, and are available all over. Alternative newsgroups do not follow the conventions, and are only available upon request.

Veronica a *gopher* tool that quickly reads through a listing of all the resources and directory titles available, then displays a list from which you can choose.

virus a *program* that can reproduce itself and spread from one program to another, or even one computer to another. Designed by evil programmers, viruses are usually meant to destroy data or otherwise disturb the computer.

WAIS see Wide Area Information Server.

Web see World Wide Web.

Wide Area Information Server also known as WAIS, and pronounced "ways," a resource for finding documents that allows you to search for them according to the words they contain, rather than the document names. This means, for example, that you can use WAIS to find documents that have the words "Panama Canal," in the text, even if those words do not appear in the title. The documents you are looking for must be in a database with which WAIS can work.

word processor a computer *program* that allows you to write and edit on your computer. Most allow you to arrange the text in columns, check spelling and hyphenation, use different fonts, etc.

World Wide Web also known as WWW and Web, a tool that allows you to *browse* through the Internet. It uses *hypertext links* that allow you to rapidly jump from document to document, even if the documents are on different computers in different countries. Point to what you want and WWW gets it for you.

Yahoo stands for "Yet Another Hierarchically Officious Oracle." Yahoo is a *subject tree* that organizes *Internet* resources into thousands of categories and subcategories. After tapping into Yahoo at http://wwwyahoocom/, you can make your choice of category or subcategory without having to know the exact term for what you want. (Other search tools require that you know how to name what you're looking for.)

Appendix

Where to get information

Online services

Here's where to contact the major online services:

America Online
8619 Westwood Center
  Drive
Vienna, VA 22182
800-827-6364

AT&T Business Network
P.O. Box 604
Fargo, ND 58107
800-265-4703

CompuServe
5000 Arlington Center
  Boulevard
Columbus, OH 43220
800-848-8199

eWorld
Apple Computer, Inc.
1 Infinite Loop Drive
Cuppertino, CA 95014
800-775-4556

Genie: General Electric
  Information Services
P.O. Box 6403
Rockville, MD 20850
800-638-9636

Prodigy
445 Hamilton Avenue
White Plains, NY 10601
800-776-0845

Books

Many books explain computer basics, including:

Plain English Computer Dictionary, Joe Kraynak, Carmel, IN: Alpha Books, 1992.

Buy That Computer!, Dan Gookin, Foster City, CA: IDG Books, 1995.

There are numerous books about the Information Superhighway and the Internet, such as:

Everything You Need to Know (But Were Afraid to Ask Kids) About the Information Highway, Merle Marsh, Ed.D., Palo Alto, CA: The Computer Learning Foundation, 1995.

How To Use the Internet 2nd ed., Marietta Tretter, Emeryville, CA: Ziff Davis Press, 1995.

Internet In Plain English. 2nd ed., Bryan Pfaffenberger, New York: MIS Press, 1996.

The Internet Guide for New Users, Daniel Dern, New York: McGraw-Hill, 1994.

The Student's Guide to Doing Research on the Internet, Dave and Mary Campbell, New York: Addison-Wesley Publishing Company, 1995.

Shelves full of books help you master the ins and outs of online services:

The Little Online Book, Alfred Glossbrenne, Berkeley, CA: Peachpit Press, 1995.

Cruising America Online, Grace Betty, David Gardner and David Sauer, Rocklin, CA: Prima, 1995.

Navigating the Internet with America Online, Wes Tatters, Indianapolis, IN: Sams.net, 1995.

The Trail Guide to Prodigy, Caroline Hallidy, New York: Addison-Wesley, 1995.

How To Use Prodigy, Douglas Hogert, Emeryville, CA: Ziff Davis Press, 1994.

CompuServe for Dummies, Wallace Wang, San Mateo, CA: IDG Books, 1994.

Welcome to CompuServe for Windows, Michael Banks, New York: MIS Press, 1994.

Internet "yellow pages"

You'll find thousands of Internet addresses in the many all-purpose Internet "yellow pages" such as:

The Internet Yellow Pages, Harly Hahn, New York: McGraw-Hill, 1996.

The Internet Directory, Eric Braun, New York: Fawcett Columbine, 1994.

What's On the Internet, Eric Gagnon, Berkeley, CA: Peachpit Press, 1994.

Netguide. 2nd ed., Kelly Maloni, Ben Greenman, Kristen Miller and Jeff Hearn, New York: Random House, 1995.

There are also Internet "yellow pages" devoted to single topics, including:

Law On the Net, James Evans, Berkeley, CA: NoLo Press, 1995.

Politics On the Web, Bill Mann, Indianapolis, IN: Que, 1995.

A Pocket Tour of Health and Fitness On the Internet, Jeanne Ryer, San Francisco, CA: Sybex, 1995.

Software manufacturers

You can contact manufacturers for information on their software. Here are the names and numbers of some leading educational software manufacturers/distributors:

ABC/EA Home Software, 800-245-4525

Against All Odds Productions, 800-588-3388, Dept. 700

Attica Cybernetics, 800-721-2475

Bayware, Inc., 800-538-8867

Bible Research Systems, 800-423-1228

Blasterware, 800-998-5227

Books That Work, 800-242-4546

Byron Preiss Multimedia, 800-910-0099

Cambrix Publishing, 800-992-8781

Claris Corp, 800-3-CLARIS

Cliff Notes, 800-228-4078

Compton's NewMedia, 800-862-2206

Corbis Publishing, 206-641-4505

Creative Multimedia, 800-262-7668

Davidson & Associates, 800-545-7677

Discovery Channel, The, 800-762-2189

DK Multimedia, 800-356-6575

Encyclopaedia Britannica, Inc., 800-323-1229

IVI Publishing, 800-952-4773

Kaplan Educational Centers, 800-KAP-ITEM

Learning Company, The, 800-852-2255

Maris Multimedia, 800-639-8717

Merriam-Webster Electronic Publishing, 800-828-1880

Microsoft Corp, 800-426-9400

Multicom Publishing, 800-850-7272

National Geographic Society, 800-647-5463

New Line Cinema, 800-294-0022

Novell, Inc., 800-451-5151

Pacific Software, 800-232-3989

Redheads Software, 800-205-9581

Software Toolworks, The, 800-845-8698

Time Warner Interactive, 800-482-3766

Vicarious, Inc., 800-465-6543

Voyager Company, The, 800-446-2001

Zane Publishing, 800-769-3723

ZCI Publishing, 800-460-2323

Index